Winning the War for College Talent

Trudy G. Steinfeld
Emanuel Contomanolis

This book is dedicated to the college recruiter — the talent acquisition professional.
To those brave souls who navigate the complex waters of higher education with its diverse institutions, processes, and cultures to find the right candidates and successfully recruit them into their organizations.
Recruiters undertake this challenge with boundless energy and enthusiasm knowing full well that they will encounter competition for the best talent at every turn; are required to constantly master new tools, technologies and processes; and face seemingly ever changing student demographics, preferences, values, interests, and cultures.

CONTENTS

Introduction and Acknowledgments

We have collaborated on so many projects blending our complementary perspectives and outlooks always, in what we hoped, was an effort to advance our profession and be of service to our colleagues. We were pleased with the success of our first book *Leadership in Career Services: Voices from the Field* and while we always planned on a second edition of that volume, it was also clear that we had another goal to accomplish first. If we really believed in advancing the work of our profession and our national association, which benefits from the receipt of all proceeds from the sales of these books, then it was important to us to make a concentrated and parallel effort to produce a volume that might address the needs and interests of our employer colleagues. This book attempts to do just that.

As always, we benefited from the enthusiastic support of the project by the National Association of College and Employers (NACE), and in particular by the encouragement of then NACE President Dawn Carter and Executive Director Marilyn. Their support was always a source of inspiration and comfort to us.

None of this would not be possible, of course, with the willingness of so many talented people to contribute their time and expertise and we want to acknowledge and thank the 33 individuals who contributed essays to the book. They were all wonderful to work with and shared our enthusiasm for this undertaking.

We would also like to thank M'Chelle Ryan of the NYU Wasserman Center for Career Development who assisted in the production of the book.

We are blessed to work in a vibrant and exciting profession and always thankful for the opportunities it presents to pursue our interests and advance our collective efforts.

Trudy G. Steinfeld and Emanuel Contomanolis

Foreword

Even as an active and seasoned talent acquisition professional, I am constantly astonished by the new technologies, innovative new practices, and fierce competition that describes our efforts in campus based talent recruiting. The enormous differences in higher education institutions, talent acquisition organizations, and effective recruiting strategies make our work both incredibly challenging and exciting. The challenge, of course, is in determining the most effective acquisition strategy that best achieves the talent goals of your organization. The excitement comes from the successful execution of that strategy and the success of your efforts.

There are many resources, partners, and service providers, eager to inform and assist our recruiting efforts. I am excited that this book can be added to the list of those valuable resources. The essays included in this volume represent a variety of helpful insights and perspectives focused specifically on campus based recruiting. It is nearly impossible to address all areas of concern in this fast-paced and rapidly changing landscape, but this volume offers important commentary on critical topics such as recruiting strategy development, school selection, diversity recruiting, employer branding, trends in college student interests and behaviors, technology, analytics and assessment, and working with campus partners. The contributors are experienced and insightful, offering helpful practical advice and setting the stage with this initial effort for further dialog and the building of interested networks and communities to advance our knowledge and expertise further.

I am particularly pleased that the editors and contributors to this book have been strong supporters of the National Association of Colleges and Employers (NACE). There is no stronger evidence of this support than their willingness to contribute to the creation of this resource and to dedicate all the proceeds from its sales to the NACE Center for Career Development and Talent Acquisition.

As Past President of NACE it was my pleasure to work with the editors by sharing my own views and perspectives and doing all I could to encourage their enthusiasm for this project. It is no easy undertaking to gather insights

---

7

from such a broad-based group of talent acquisition leaders, and I truly appreciate their promise to complete the project. For that I am very grateful.

Please enjoy reviewing the contents of this book and successfully applying the insights you might gain to your own efforts.

Dawn Carter
Past President, NACE
Director, Early Careers at Intuit

Winning the "War" for College Talent

Morgan Hoogevelt

For those of you who are movie enthusiasts, John Rambo once said, "To win at war…one must become war" and this is exactly the mindset one must employ if you want to succeed and ultimately win in the competitive landscape for talent in Corporate America. While the majority of Corporate America continues to fight over experienced and developed professionals; there is an untapped pool of fresh and hungry college graduates looking to enter the workforce and get their feet wet inside Corporate America.

Those companies and organizations that recognize and "fish in this pool", can reap great rewards in acquiring talent. And to the naysayers who continue to believe the overhype and disparaging remarks of the new generation (millennials); I personally believe that talk is all hogwash as people are as good as their leaders allow them to be, regardless of age and generation. When recruiting College Graduates there are several basic keys one should practice in order to be successful in winning the "war" for collegiate talent. Hopefully you will find one or two takeaways that you can immediately implement if you are not doing so already; or perhaps there are things you can build on within your own portfolio of skills when it comes to recruiting college graduates.

Here are the tips I recommend you follow and execute…

1. **Know and target the right universities** – I receive more calls and emails than I can count from various universities marketing their career fairs and networking events. It's very easy for me to sign up, pack up my career fair gear, and head out to spend a few hours at the local university talking to students. But rather than just sign up and show up; do your research and find out what universities offer majors and programs geared to the relevant roles you hope to fill. This sounds like a trivial first tip, but in my time of attending career fairs; I have met more employers than I care to remember who, when I ask them what skill sets they are seeking, they reply, "Anything and everything" (I'm not sure what that means). Many universities all

over the country are now partnering with Fortune 500 companies to establish specialty programs and majors. So perhaps you want to recruit Junior Analyst's – maybe you look for a school that has a Big Data major.

In a past role of mine, I had recruited entry level sales individuals and through some research, believe it or not; there are multiple universities out there that now offer Sales majors and there is even an annual event called the Sales Olympics that hosts, trains and develops college students to be sales professionals and to compete against each other. So, do your research, find out what schools will be most beneficial to your needs and then specifically target those universities and their students.

2. **Go straight to the source** – One of the most important activities that you can engage in needs to be done well before setting foot on a campus – and that is building, maintaining and cultivating relationships with the Professors. Yes…you heard me right, have a relationship with the Professors. Think about it, the high majority of your competition will not do this; they will simply receive the email from the local Student Services office, send in their check for the $250 entrance fee, and then show up on career day with a fancy table and trinkets while sitting behind the desk texting their friends. So, I challenge you to target the relevant schools and then start a relationship with the faculty members.

The Professors know everything that's happening on campus, especially when it comes to the students. They know who shows up to class, who puts in the time and effort, who studies, who has the grades and who possesses the ability to be a stellar employee. They'll also know the students who never show up, who don't put in the time and effort and frankly…they'll know the ones you want to stay clear away from. Great students will have strong relationships with their professors and communicate with them regularly. Students trust their professors and their opinions, ideas and recommendations. Get in good with a faculty members and build strong relationships – you will find yourself with a continuous stream of strong student referrals.

If you can master this relationship tip with campus faculty, you will be at the forefront of the competition and find yourself working smarter and not harder.

3. **Be bold** - When I attend career fairs, hiring conferences, recruiting events, or through conversations with prospective candidates, I've learned that at times, the wrong people are attending these events as recruiters. Many of the professionals that attend career fairs are unable to communicate at a level that would properly represent their company.

    The behavior I've witnessed at these types of events are predictive of how these recruiters behave in the office and how they represent their company through other communication tools such as social media. I witnessed these individuals sitting behind their tables, eating food, talking on cell phones, and displaying body language that suggested they didn't want to be bothered.

    Fortunately, I've witnessed several individuals and companies that did exhibit proper career fair behavior and strong recruiting traits. They were the ones that had long lines of candidates and also the ones whose companies are always recognized as recruiting industry leaders. The difference in success was clear; majority of graduating college students may not know who your company is, let alone what it does. So be assertive and bold; step out from behind the table and invite your prospects to become familiar with your company if they aren't already. Share the information with them knowing they are new at this job search thing. Most importantly…ask them what they are seeking and what they want to do in their professional life. After all, this is more about them and less about you.

    If you really want to go the extra mile, be personable and share your contact information and avenues of research for the students so they can perform their due diligence on your company and opportunities. You can even go as far as to collect a group of prospective candidates and invite them all to your company and provide them a tour or a meet and greet with key Executives and business leaders. The more you can share about your company and opportunities…you will

11

create excitement, interest and passion, which equals you beating your competition.

4. **Build a network** – if you haven't realized this, Collegiate Alumni groups are ultra-powerful and groups of young motivated professionals can be equally as powerful; especially with today's social media networks. So, keep in touch with interns and new college graduate hires and use them as 'recruiters' for future talent. Who better to accompany a recruiter at a collegiate career fair than a recent intern or a new graduate that recently made the cut and can share their story?

Companies forget about this wealth of valuable talent that can be leveraged to their advantage and help them recruit more successfully. Through speaking with these recent college hires or interns, you can gain valuable market information as to what groups are on campus, what events students participate in and invite yourself to speak and network with these groups. Getting yourself in front of the prospects early on and being able to share information and potential career paths will be extremely valuable for your recruitment efforts.

5. **Interviewing** – once you identify those potential candidates that you want to interview, it is of utmost importance that you have the interview process buttoned up, hiring managers briefed and strive for a great candidate experience. Build an interview panel of people who have had fairly recent experiences, people with longevity, and with people that can provide good prospective on the job and company. Have them meet the team members, provide them a tour where you can showcase the company gym, the café or even the break room with the ping pong table. Some of these things may seem trivial to you and I; but to new college graduates these things could make the world of difference in selecting an employer.

Lastly, if you want to make a strong impression while building some comradery with the interviewee and the group; hold part of the interview over lunch in a relaxed setting to really get to know the person and vice versa. You'll see a different side of the candidate and they'll see a different side of the interview team in a semi relaxed environment while enjoying some good food and conversation.

6. **The experience** – two main points: first - hiring someone is not a "set it and forget it" exercise and second – news travels like wild fire in today's social media world. It's of most importance that you have your new hire and onboarding process buttoned up in order to ensure the new hire has a great experience and first impression, first day and first week.

Fresh college grads will ask what you may think are the silly questions; however, put yourself back in their shoes and remember your Day 1 at your first ever job. They will need to know where to park, what time to show up, what to wear, what door to enter, where they can place their lunch, etc. I clearly recall a new hire we made several years ago, let's call him Ralph. Ralph stopped in on the Friday before his Monday start date to drop off his new hire paperwork. I patiently waited for him in the lobby to arrive and greeted him with a big smile, a firm handshake and a warm welcome (I was determined to create a great candidate experience). Ralph and I exchanged brief conversation about his weekend plans, I accepted his new hire paperwork and then I wished him well and that I would see him on Monday.   As I turned to walk back to my office and turn in his paperwork, I heard a timid and faint, "Oh Sir…uh…may I ask you a question…?" I turned to Ralph and saw a look of confusion on his face and replied, "Sure, ask away", totally not prepared for what he was going to ask me. "Well Sir…where should I park? And should I bring my lunch; and where can I put it?" I took a step back at the situation and it dawned on me as trivial as I thought those questions were, this was Ralph's first time in his adult life that he ever stepped foot inside Corporate America.

Take heed to this and make sure you have your new hire all set up and ready to go for Day 1; but don't stop there. Make sure your new hire has a work station and that it's set up with the necessary equipment and supplies. Take them on a tour and make introductions and get them acquainted with the business and their coworkers. Schedule a lunch as kind of a "Welcome to the Company" celebration and build some comradery between the new person and the veterans. Ensure this person has meaningful work to do and that they receive the proper training they need in order to accomplish the tasks you set out for them. Most important…continue to check up with them and let them know how they are doing, what they need from you and that you are taking in any ideas and allowing them to contribute; because after all, while they may be new to the working world – you hired them to be another expert in their profession.

A negative onboarding and week one experience will leave rippling effects as the experience will be shared via social media channels, on GlassDoor and with their former classmates and Professors. News like that will surely turn off others who have your company on their radar and this is what you want to avoid at all costs.

In today's human capital climate, talent continues to be deemed as 'scarce' and 'not available'. I'm here to counter that and tell you that there is plenty of talent available in both experienced professionals and new college graduates. You just have to apply basic principles like the ones I shared with you here, build relationships and be proactive to go out and stand out, in order to win the talent game. I love sports as it is my passion; and every time a new season kicks off, be it MLB, NBA or the NFL…the players always start with spring training, spring work outs or pre-season practice. Why? They go back to the basics and start by practicing the most rudimentary techniques like throwing the baseball to first base, hitting a receiver on a 20-yard post pattern or by practicing free throws.

We in Corporate America have come to rely on technology and systems to hunt talent and have become so desensitized to conversation, interaction and to the basics, that in a lot of cases, we have forgotten how to execute on human to human behavior. But if we can go back to the basics in a lot of what we do as recruiters and apply logic and common sense and remember that a human touch will go a long way; it is then that you will win the "War for College Talent".

Trends & Predictions for College Talent Programs

Marilyn Mackes

In a fast-paced environment with daily headlines and info bytes on predictive analytics and data-driven business strategies, we face a continuous challenge to understand the external framework and trends for building college talent programs. Why do these trends matter so much? By identifying trends, we …

- Become aware of the larger environmental context within which we must operate and are better prepared to respond to it and plan based on it.
- Anticipate and act based on what we expect the future will hold rather than merely reacting to external factors as they arise.
- Engage in a strategic approach to sourcing, developing and retaining talent based on the implications of trends and a future-focused perspective.
- Gain insights on opportunities for change and improvement of our talent program strategies and action plans.

More than ever before, positioning organizations for successful talent acquisition, development and retention programs depends on awareness of the external landscape, understanding data and recruitment benchmarks, and acknowledging future drivers that will impact strategy.

Landscape trends

Economic

In recent years and for the near term most economists see the U.S. and global economies continuing to experience growth at approximately 2.5% GDP. We are not currently operating within a context of a global financial crisis nor are we seeing unlimited expansion in global markets. There are concerns about the implications for changes in trade agreements, global investments and cross-border activities. Overall, economists project a cautiously positive outlook. It is imperative, however, to note that there is no crystal ball to predict the economic implications of a national or global crisis. As employers plan talent acquisition strategy, the economic landscape trends for their geographic targets will play a vital role.

Higher Education

Within higher education, the source for college talent, a number of key trends provide a backdrop for understanding strategic priorities for institutions as they plan for the future and for employers as they plan for engagement in university programs. Studies produced by higher education association leaders highlight the following areas for special concern and attention:

- Diversity Enrollment
- Affordability of Higher Education & Funding the Student
- Access to Education
- Skills Gap
- International Students
- Graduate Outcomes Data
- Institutional Performance Metrics

Employers clearly share some of these same priorities, affording opportunities for stronger connections between institutions and employers to address common interests.

Employers

Of particular focus for employers are a number of talent management trends that have implications for how organizations plan and implement their recruitment and hiring strategies.

Candidate Experience

A number of recent studies reveal the importance and value of employers providing a positive candidate experiences during the application process. A study by Workplacetrends.com found that approximately 60% of job seekers have had a poor candidate experience and the majority of candidates are now sharing this information through online review sites. Criticism is focused on lack of responsiveness, delayed timeframes for communication and "dehumanizing" processes. A SHRM study has indicated that nearly 40% of employers are investing in the improvement of the candidate experience. Inc.com recently profiled one such company, Virgin Media, for its new approach to treat candidates like customers. Their approach states, "What if your candidate experience was so positive that it created new customer acquisition opportunities from people we have engaged with?" With this in mind, we are likely to see more internal collaboration among customer service/marketing/human resource professionals as they view their prospective employees as potential customers.

Diversity

According to *LinkedIn Global Recruiting Trends 2017,* building programs and resources for achieving a diverse workforce is one of the top three trends for future talent management. This need across all industry sectors and geographies drives a mandate that affects all employers. According to a SHRM study of recruitment activity, 57% of recruiters have focused responsibilities related to diversity recruitment. The focus on developing and sourcing a diverse workforce is shared by both higher educational institutions and employers and will likely lead to more collaborative partnerships to achieve this common goal.

Mobile & Social Access

With the mainstreaming of "social recruitment" and the ubiquitous use of mobile devices, many recruiting employers are saying "mobile first" as their priority for branding, candidate communication and application. Employers regularly implement new technology tools to ensure they are gaining access to today's generation of student candidates. According to LinkedIn, 72% of job candidates visit the employer mobile site to explore employment options and 45% are applying using mobile devices. These numbers are likely only to increase as we look ahead.

Analytics

In recent years, employers have explored insights provided through analysis of "Big Data" and the advantages it can provide for predictive analytics supporting talent management. The *2017 Deloitte Global Human Capital Trends* report highlights the need to "rewrite the rules for a digital age." In particular, two trends relate to analytics: 1) "Digital HR" as it relates to technology-based platforms and the digital workforce and 2) "People Analytics," using data for determining business strategy and solutions. Other studies by SHRM and LinkedIn confirm that more organizations are looking to expand the use of analytics for workforce planning, recruitment, development and retention.

Blended Workforce

With the rise of the "sharing economy," increased demands for flexible work roles and the growth of freelancers working multiple "gigs," many experts predict the workforce of the future will be a blended mix of the traditional employee and contingency workers. Korn Ferry's *2017 Talent Trend Predictions* produced by the Futurestep Division noes that some think that by 2020 we may see independent contractors comprising 40% of the American workforce. Even now we see employers developing "flexible teams" of freelancers working with employees on shared projects. More employers are currently hiring "on-demand" to meet particular time-sensitive needs. While college graduates have historically engaged in more traditional employment arrangements, we are likely to see changes here both in terms of expectations of the candidates for flexible employment options as well for employers leveraging the advantages of the blended workforce.

NACE Research and Benchmarks

NACE has a long history of gathering data from employers and job candidates to provide insights regarding recruiting and employment related trends. In recent years, we have seen significant shifts in practices as well as expectations. It is not surprising to see the research data around college talent supporting the trends already noted for the larger employment marketplace.

Employer Benchmarks
- Diversity: More than 70% have formal programs in place
- Social Media: 68% use for branding and recruiting
- Video Interviews: 55% include in selection process (numbers increasing each year)
- Internships: 65% prefer new hires with experience

Employer Preferences
As described in studies by SHRM, LinkedIn, Deloitte, Forbes and many others, preferred skills and competencies have become a central theme for employers sourcing college talent. In the *NACE 2016 Recruiting Benchmarks Survey*, employers identified skills and competencies most critical in their assessment of candidates:
- Decision making and problem solving
- Teamwork
- Communication: verbal and written
- Plan, organize, and prioritize work

- Obtain and process information
- Analyze quantitative data
- Technical knowledge of the job
- Proficiency with computer software programs
- Sell to or influence others

In looking at the *NACE 2016 Student Survey* we can see complementary data regarding the use of technology platforms, social media, participation in internships and their preferences for their future full-time work experiences.

Student Benchmarks

- Primary Sources: websites, career services, social media, personal contacts
- Tools: mobile devices
- Social Media: >86% use LinkedIn and >50% are comfortable with employers contacting them via social media
- Internships: > 60% held internships/co-ops
- Entering the Workforce: >85% consider themselves career ready

Student Preferences

NACE has been tracking criteria for students' preferences when assessing employer options for more than ten years. Over that time students have identified different preferences depending on environmental influences and issues – i.e. corporate downsizing, increase of start-ups, etc. Student perspectives over the past five years have revealed an increasing interest in their individual personal development as the following list demonstrates.

Personal Growth	56%
Friendly Work Environment	42%
Job Security	41%
Benefits	37%
Contribute to Community	33%

Salary	19%
Location	17%
"Green" Company	9%

Interestingly, as the numbers below confirm, personal growth is also the highest rated preference across all disciplines.

- Business – 69.8%
- Engineering & Science – 58.3%
- Humanities – 56.9%
- Social Sciences – 52.5%

As employers consider attracting talent into their organizations it will be critical to communicate how new hires will be able to develop and strengthen their experiences and capabilities.

Future drivers

Of the many predictions about the future of talent acquisition, three in particular are already in motion and noteworthy for employers to consider as they prepare for what lies ahead.

AI (Artificial Intelligence) technology: revolutionizing talent management

Personal assistants, embedded virtual reality and cognitive technologies have now become mainstream in our daily lives and will soon be implemented more pervasively within organizations as automated sourcing, hiring and training tools. According to a SHRM study one-fourth of employers ranked automated sourcing tools as the top trend shaping the recruiting industry during the next five to ten years. Deloitte's Global Trends survey reported that 41% of employers have either implemented or will soon be adopting cognitive and AI technologies, with 35% reporting pilot programs in place. In addition, employing organizations are looking closely at the value of augmented reality tools for employee training. Challenges? Besides the obvious one related to transition from people-operated to machine-based functions, how will these new developments impact the demand for improving the candidate experience? Opportunities? College graduates have engaged in virtual reality games and activities for years and, as a Forbes report tells us, one-fourth of gen Z and millennials would like to see companies bring virtual reality into the workplace.

Real-time learning and teams: A new model for professional development

Many companies are embracing the concept that employees are engaged in a range of experiences that enable them to acquire and strengthen skills on their own terms. This is particularly significant within a context that includes a more limited life-span of technical skills, a blended workforce that includes increasing numbers of people working remotely and the range of self-directed learning options both inside and outside organizations. More companies are also acknowledging the value of high performing teams, restructuring with the intent to increase thought leadership capacity and competitiveness. Deloitte reports that 83% of corporate executives rate "careers and learning" as important for their future talent management plans. NACE research mirrors other national studies that identify teamwork and collaboration high on the list of skills employers prefer. Challenges? How will organizations adapt to the concept of professional development "owned" by the individual who can design it themselves? How will the growing numbers of people working remotely and through contingent arrangements become effectively engaged in organizational team structures? Opportunities? Integrating the value of self-driven learning with team engagement could present new opportunities for professionals to experience an "always learning" approach, a concept some believe is far better than a hierarchical, highly structured learning program. Teams, of course, will continue to create opportunities for the richness of diverse thinking and shared commitment and responsibility.

Culture and the employee experience: Impact on talent retention

What do you envision when you see these words: communal workplace, artisanal education, vagabond headquarters, jeans –the new business casual, wellness center, hoteling, flex scheduling? There was a time when these reflected the exception for what employers provide for their employees. That is no longer the case. Google Trends data reports that the term "employee experience" has jumped 140% since 2011. According to LinkedIn, employers are moving toward more personalization in the workplace in terms of benefits, compensation, work location and overall operations. They are viewing the "employee journey," analyzing the needs of the workforce within the context of personal well-being, workplace design and productivity. Challenges? Culture change is extremely difficult and with five generations in the workforce, employers are working to meet the expectations of a broad range of employees. How can organizations identify and then implement those offerings of particular value to their employees? Opportunities? If employees feel engaged, challenged and valued, strong retention will result.

Positioning for the Future

Employers looking to proactively and strategically plan for what lies ahead in acquiring and retaining college talent may want to explore these critical questions:

1. What forms of innovative disruption, revolution or evolution are you observing or experiencing?
2. How will these changes impact your future college talent acquisition, development and retention strategies?

References:

Adams, B. "How Richard Branson Plans to Make Over $7Million a Year from … Recruiting?" Inc.com, June 20, 2016.

Bersin, J. "9 HR Tech Trends for 2017." Shrm.org, January 25, 2017.

Chamberlain, A. "Looking Ahead: 5 Jobs Trends to Watch in 2017." Glassdoor.com, December 15, 2016.

Deloitte. *2017 Deloitte Global Human Capital Trends.* Deloitte University Press. 2016.

Economist, The. *The World in 2017.* November 2016.

Gutsche, J. *Top 20 Trends in 2017*. Trendreports.com, December 2, 2016.

Korn Ferry Futurestep. "Korn Ferry Futurestep Makes 2017 Talent Trend Predictions." Kornfery.com, December 13, 2016.

LinkedIn Talent Blog. *Global Recruiting Trends 2017*. November 11, 2016.

Min, Ji-A. "The Top 3 Recruiting Trends of 2017." Rework, Cornerstoneondemand.com, December 21, 2016.

National Association of Colleges and Employers (2016). *2016 Recruiting Benchmarks Survey*. January 2017.

National Association of Colleges and Employers (2016). *The Class of 2016 Student Survey*. October 2016.

Schwabel, D. (2016) "10 Workplace Trends You'll See in 2017." Forbes.com, November 1, 2016.

Schwabel, D. (2016) "Candidate Experience Study." Workplacetrends.com, June 14, 2016.

Thirteen Components of a Strategic Campus Recruiting Program

John Flato

As one who has consulted with employers in the campus recruiting industry, I have received numerous requests to help employers develop a *"strategic" campus recruiting program.* I have led the campus recruiting function at AlliedSignal (now known as Honeywell), Cigna, and Ernst & Young, and served as the Director of Career Services at Georgetown's McDonough MBA School. I have consulted with more than 60 clients over the past ten years, and have a network of university relations professionals and career center leaders. I also asked many of my friends in the industry: what constitutes a strategic program? What follows is a compilation of their responses to my question about strategic programs, with my analysis.

The components of what makes a program strategic include:

1. The business case for a program is well defined, articulated, and embraced by the enterprise

The first question I ask a prospective client is why they want to initiate a college recruiting program. Developing a strategic program is no small task, nor is it inexpensive. I ask if they have identified or established the business imperatives for creating such a program. Here are some of the reasons for creating a university recruiting program:

The company or employer:
- Is growing and needs entry level talent to fulfill new roles;
- Is experiencing voluntary or involuntary turnover;
- Has an aging workforce with retirements looming, and needs talent to replace those who will be leaving;
- Needs to innovate and is looking for hires who are able to develop and use the new technologies being taught in colleges today;
- Wants to be recognized as an employer that hires at entry level and promotes from within;

- Wants to reduce costs for expensive search fees or simply replace higher salaries with entry level salaries of new campus graduates;
- Would like to improve its diversity and inclusion metrics by recruiting more diverse talent from campus;
- Wants to change workplace culture by hiring new employees who don't perpetuate an existing work culture or bring bad habits with them.

Whatever the reasons for starting a new or improving an existing program, the business case must be fully understood and embraced by senior management, in order to obtain the needed resources and commitment to conduct a successful program.

2. *Senior executives actively support, advocate, and participate in the recruiting process*

The organizations that truly stand out in terms of campus recruiting are those that not only have executive support for a robust program, but whose executives actively participate in campus recruiting events. If talent acquisition (specifically, getting the best candidates to apply and accept) is important to the enterprise, there are roles that senior executives should play. Campus recruiting is more than just a Human Resources responsibility. Using executives effectively provides the company visibility, distinguishes it to the faculty and administration, helps to reinforce its employment brand, and sends the message that the employer is committed to acquiring talent and wants the best to join. Large banks, professional service firms, and some manufacturing companies use their executives quite extensively in their recruitment efforts.

Ways to engage the company's most senior executives include:
- Have them serve as a Campus Executive at a university leading the school strategy and the campus team.
- Serve on an advisory board or committee at the university.
- Have them interact with students and take greater ownership of the process by delivering the company's recruiting presentation.
- Have them help to "close the deal" by personally call candidates from the schools they visited to extend an offer

- Engage them in various events on campus such as judging contests or speaking at intern events.

If the most senior executives in the university recruiting process, they should receive a training program so that they fully understand what is expected of them and the time commitment. They should be kept abreast of the progress at their respective universities, such that they feel that they have "skin in the game."

3. Jobs for new grads are developmental and appeal to the millennial generation

The Millennial generation needs to feel wanted and special. Generally speaking, they need to feel that they are entering into a role that will challenge them and that they will have leaders who support their development. Before sourcing them, it's important to determine what competencies or soft skills are in demand beyond the technical job-specific skills, who will train the new hires on their role, and what will prepare new grads for the future. Too often, I'll read job descriptions that state merely a job title and qualifications that are being sought, like a grade point average, work experience, and other requirements. Often there is no element that will appeal to new graduates, whether that's work-life balance, interesting projects, or other triggers that resonate with this new generation of student. Companies that provide the "WIFM" factor, that is, "what's in it for me?" answer the questions on the minds of the candidates.

In terms of creating jobs for new campus graduates, consider including the following in the job description on your career portal as well as other job announcements:

- What are the specific job responsibilities, not just the requirements to obtain the job.
- Where will this job lead? In other words, what are the growth and development opportunities?
- What are the differentiators you might offer new college graduates? How are you addressing student specific student desires (such as flexible working hours, casual dress, and other factors)?

Some employers answer these questions directly on their websites, on job announcements and in presentations. Most new graduates are looking for a career, not just a job. Companies that can articulate that differentiation are those that appeal to the best students.

4. Key schools are identified and strong relationships are developed at each

School selection for recruiting purposes is very controversial and emotional, as there are historical connections to some universities, they may be the alma mater of some of your executives, and other factors. There is no doubt that in order to maximize a company's financial and human resources, there should be a set of key schools from which the employer recruits the bulk of its interns and full-time candidates.

Organizations that recruit new graduates, conduct research, and provide philanthropic support at the same set of institutions will be even better off. The philosophy that I have brought to the companies that I've worked for and consulted to is that "it is better to be a bigger player at few schools, than a bit player at a lot of schools." There is no doubt that there is exceptional talent at virtually every college and university in the country, but from an efficiency basis, I advocate for a targeted school approach with a concentrated effort. Criteria for school selection will be covered elsewhere in this book, but it's important to note that data should be gathered from internal and external sources. Having a sound, data-driven selection process will prevent recruiting from schools that may be unwise uses of company resources.

5. The recruiting process is flawless and repeatable year after year: "Everything starts with a numeric goal"

One of the key benefits of a campus recruiting process is that it reoccurs on a relatively standard basis each year. The most important element of effective recruiting is obtaining hiring goals for full-time positions and internships well before an employer first steps foot on campus. This sounds easy, but it has been my experience that goal-setting can be one of the most difficult components of the campus recruiting process. I have also encountered a significant reluctance to potentially over-hire, that is, make more offers than there are vacant positions. I think of this recruiting practice as "vacancy driven" rather than "strategy driven." The organizations that have the most successful campus recruiting programs will make expeditious offers to convert interns to full-time employees, as well as those they interview on campus. Best practice companies use a time-tested formula, recognizing that not all offers will be accepted. If the company receives a better than anticipated acceptance rate, the "over-hires" will be accommodated.

A solid hiring plan will dictate:

- How many schools a company will recruit from,
- How many recruiting schedules it will need,
- How many people must be trained as interviewers and/or supervisors,
- How much merchandise the company will need to purchase,
- How many on-site interview dates will need to be scheduled.

I suggest getting that data no later than May of any calendar year.

Campus recruiting processes need year-round attention; it's not just a fall and spring activity. Designing and refining a strategy, reporting on progress, training those involved in interviewing and supervision, developing relationships, scheduling events, and so much more can be put in an annual calendar that spans across the enterprise such that everyone involved knows their role and time commitments.

6. Co-op and intern programs are used appropriately: "Interns are a means to an end, not an end in and of itself"

I speak to many leaders in the campus recruiting community and am constantly surprised that intern programming doesn't necessarily lead to a high conversion into full-time roles. It's important to consider this when planning an internship program. Here are my six recommended purposes of an intern program:

- **Screen interns for full-time positions, and offer them jobs upon the completion of the internship.** The internship should serve as an 8-12 week-long interview. This should be the primary purpose of an intern program.
- **Use the interns as your ambassadors when they return to campus.** One of the primary ways that students find out about what it's like to work at a company is to talk to employees or

former employees, like interns. Using your interns strategically when they return to campus, to promote your brand, identify classmates who would be of interest to your company, and advertise your appearances on campus are just a few ways the best managed programs use their interns.

- **Get real work done that might otherwise not get accomplished**. There are usually back-burner projects, people on vacation, and other reasons that interns are needed to perform work that might not get done. Hiring interns is a great way to give them exposure to these types of projects while also accomplishing real progress within a company.
- **Build a diversity pipeline**. Many companies develop a robust intern program that focuses on attracting diverse candidates who can be converted into full-time hires.
- **Save the company money**. Interns get paid less than contractors and full-time employees. Getting work accomplished using interns is an excellent way to spread your brand, while accomplishing many of the goals stated above.
- **Community and Employee Relations**: Some companies will give back to their local communities by offering internships and summer jobs to students from the community. Some companies offer what's known as "friends and family" opportunities for children of employees, and while these internships are not given with the intention of converting interns to full-time hires, they are a way to engage with current employees.

Many of the best practice companies are using their intern programs to source candidates for 50-100% of their full-time hiring goal. Some companies will not hire graduating students who have not interned with them. Converting the best interns should be the *primary* source for a company's recruiting efforts.

7. *Campus recruiting efforts are coordinated with the right people involved and trained: "You only have one chance to make a first impression."*

It's critical for companies to think about their recruiting programs from the perspectives of the students and the university partners. There is nothing more confusing to the career centers and students than having different divisions of a company recruiting on separate days or using separate tables at a career fair. This sends the message that the company is not coordinated. It could also send the message that interested students must interview at each division, which is problematic at larger universities that limit the number of interviews a student might obtain through on-campus recruiting. The best-practice employers will coordinate recruiting days and career fair participation so as to maximize their firm's exposure while reducing the necessity to interview multiple times in a first-round process. There is no question that using the *right* people in the company's presentations and interview process is a key differentiator in the recruiting process. Employees who demonstrate passion and interest in students' success, who have excellent communication skills and love their employer, make a real difference in influencing impressionable students. In terms of interviewing, ensure that your representatives have been trained to screen candidates, and you should track their throughput to validate that their participation in on-campus recruiting is yielding hires. Finally, reward and recognize those who do outstanding jobs in recruiting college students and selecting the best candidates.

8. *Metrics are aggregated and routinely reported to management*

Managing a campus recruiting function is no different than managing any other department in an organization. That said, campus recruiting resources may be limited, and decision-making must be made on facts rather than emotion (or by simply doing what was done in the past). Some of the standard metrics that most companies use are ratios; how many people need to be interviewed or screened to yield a hire for example. These are called funnel statistics, where ratios are established at each level of the funnel (first-round interview, second round interview, offer, and acceptance), such that a recruiting plan can be adequately planned. Additionally, there are intern conversion rates, school by school ratios, cost-per-hire statistics, interviewer metrics, diversity tracking, source of hire, social media tracking, and much more. I advise companies to establish metrics goals prior to the recruiting season that can reasonably be tracked, and to report progress to management routinely, i.e. monthly, quarterly, and annually.

9. The campus recruiting program is adequately structured, funded, and resourced

If talent acquisition is a high priority for an employer, the campus recruiting program must be adequately resourced. There is no standard size or budget in industry, and there are many internal decisions that must be made in order to determine what is best.

Here are some fundamental factors:

- **Structure**: How will campus recruiting and relationships be organized?
  - o Centralized: funded centrally with a staff and recruiters
  - o Decentralized: each business unit and function funds recruiting from their respective budgets
  - o Hybrid: a combination of centralized services and those from the operating units and functions.
- **Budgets**: Which department(s) will fund campus recruiting?
  - o Funding may come from a combination of corporate HR, business unit or functional departments, central research, diversity and inclusion, communication/public relations and the philanthropic or foundation office.
- **Resources**: Who will perform the on-campus recruitment and associated activities?
  - o Most line staff from the business units and functions will supplement the full-time campus recruiting team. In any scenario, everyone must be trained in their roles.

Where campus recruiting goals are significantly high, employers may have budgets that exceed $1 million or more. Most companies, however, have nowhere near that amount to spend. That said, it is crucial to obtain the necessary commitments, financial and human resources to perform the tasks necessary to be successful.

10. Customer feedback is acquired and taken into account

Continuous improvement is simply a matter of good business practices. This is no different from any other department or process in a company's structure. Understanding what has worked and where there are opportunities for improvement are matters that should be considered. The easiest way to obtain customer feedback is to survey your various constituencies.

Surveys should be given to:

- Offerees (those to whom you extended an offer of employment)—why did you accept or decline the offer? If you accepted, what were the deciding factors? If you declined, where did you decide to go instead and why? How did our compensation package compare? What could we do better from a process standpoint?

- Interns—what did you like most about the internship? What could have been improved? How was the supervision you received? Would you accept an offer if it was extended? If not, why not? What did you think about the social activities we planned for you? How were your living conditions for the summer?

- Hiring managers—what did you think about the recruiting processes we deployed this year? How could they be improved? What did you think about the quality of candidates you saw this recruiting season? How did they compare to previous years?

- Candidates in the recruiting process—how have our communications to you been received? Were the logistics well organized? Did you have any problems getting to or from our facilities? Was the hotel you stayed in satisfactory?

The most important factor of collecting the data is not simply to obtain information or metrics, but to take the information, process it, and improve upon all components of the processes, logistics, administration, and other elements within control.

11. Post-offer processes are used to keep the candidates engaged

There is often an exceptionally long period between when a candidate accepts an offer immediately after an internship or even fall recruiting, and when the candidate starts his or her job. Employers that do an excellent job in recruiting are extremely adept at what's known as "candidate care" in order to keep candidates engaged—especially those who have accepted offers of employment. Companies can do a variety of things to ensure that candidates do not renege on an offer, which has been increasing in recent years. Companies with aggressive candidate care programs will send gift bags or merchandise during exam or breaks, and invite candidates to participate in company webinars or the holiday party. Some of the best managed programs will assign a "buddy" or "peer advisor" to the candidate to keep them interested and enthusiastic about the employer. Companies can also give projects for the soon-to-be employee to provide them a head start on their role while getting real work accomplished. There are many ways to keep candidates committed to the company. Those that ignore the candidate in the period between their acceptance and their on-boarding program might find themselves in difficult or embarrassing positions with the hiring managers.

12. Branding and recruitment collateral are current and relevant to students

It's often very easy to find information about employers, just like reviews of restaurants, hotels, and doctors. In order to for an employer to compete, information about employers must be easily obtained; relevant, credible, and attractive to the audience; and distinctive from other employers. The use of digital and print media is discussed in a separate chapter of this book. Suffice it to say that there are a variety of social channels that should be addressed, like Facebook, Instagram, YouTube, and LinkedIn. Information conveyed on each channel should not simply be a rehash of what is on the company website, but specifically designed for each channel. Universum's survey of more than 80,000 college students in the US, indicated that students use eight sources of media for their research of employers, and companies must be current and responsive on each channel.

13. Diversity and inclusion is a key component of the campus recruiting program

In my opinion, if diversity and inclusion is important to an employer, there is no better way to fee the pipeline than from campus. This can be accomplished by picking schools and universities where there are significant numbers of target candidates. Another way to achieve this is by accessing active clubs and associations, like the National Association of Black Accountants or the Society of Women Engineers, for example. It's important to acknowledge that many competitors are targeting these schools or associations as well, so simply recruiting at an Historically Black College and University or attending a diversity-related career fair will not yield the desired results—this will require significant, year-round efforts. It is my perspective, recruiting diverse talent from campus is more advantageous than attempting to identify experienced candidates. University recruiting allows an employer to discern the quality of education at the universities, to obtain the graduation numbers from public sources, and to become familiar with the clubs and associations to best target their efforts. Further, employers can "try before they buy," by offering internships that allow for mutual evaluations.

Final thoughts

Campus recruiting can be fun and challenging. Doing it well, however, requires a lot of effort and understanding, long-term commitments, relationship building, communication, and difficult decisions. Campus recruiting is more of a relationship-building exercise than recruiting experienced candidates. Nevertheless, obtaining talent from campus and promoting from within will be elements that may separate your firm from the rest, and truly make your company an "employer of choice."

Building and Maximizing the Recruiting Team

Dan Black

Execution: it's where the proverbial rubber meets the road. It's been proven time and time again that the best laid plans and strategies are rendered useless without laser focus on successfully and consistently implementing them. In University Relations and Recruiting (URR), execution is dependent on a host of factors including the level of leadership support, financial investment, effective use of technology, and strength of relationships, to name a few. But it is the recruiting team--broadly defined--that has the single biggest impact on the successful execution of a talent acquisition strategy. That is why I've spent the better part of two decades learning how to build, manage, motivate and develop recruiters and others involved in the recruiting process, and why I believe it's worth the time and attention of anyone serious about a career in this field. To assist with that effort, I've compiled a collection of insights from around the profession that addresses three of the most critical components of recruiting teams: the recruiters themselves, the broader talent acquisition complement, and trends that are shaping the future in this space.

Campus recruiters

When I first joined the Campus Recruiting team at EY (Ernst & Young, LLP), I can distinctly remember seeking out the advice of other, more senior professionals in Human Resources (HR). I was, after all, an accountant by training, and I wanted to get a sense for what I was getting myself into. Much of what I heard came as little surprise to me: that I'd need to work hard, that there would be good days and bad, and that I'd have a chance to make meaningful impact in the lives of other professionals. But one person I spoke to suggested something that was surprising to me; specifically, that being a campus recruiter was only a "first step" in HR and not something people typically make a career out of. I've since heard that same sentiment many times from many different people but I still feel the same way today that I did back then: it simply isn't true. In fact, a career in campus recruiting/URR is something that has become increasingly more commonplace since I joined the profession in the late 1990s. I can certainly understand where the original sentiment came from; anyone who has staffed a career fair booth or interviewed 15 or more students in a day knows the wear and tear that comes with job. The key is establishing the right options and career paths so that recruiters can grow and advance through the profession. And that begins with setting up the right structure.

Let me begin by saying that there is no one "right" way to structure your URR function. I've seen companies enjoy success using a wide variety of configurations, whether the structure and reporting lines are centralized or local, regardless of where recruiting sits in the HR organization. There are however, a few structural elements that I believe are critical success factors that should be taken into consideration in the vast majority of companies and organizations. Chief among these is the fact that the role of recruiter should be a *professional* one, not administrative. There are many ways to manage the administrative components of the URR function; and assigning those tasks to recruiting coordinators, relying on a shared services center or engaging a Recruiting Process Outsourcing (RPO) service are among the most popular. The recruiter can then function as a business partner, or at the very least a subject matter expert, helping the organization understand the talent landscape and making it possible to consistently source top talent regardless of market conditions. And while some organizations empower their line employees to serve in this capacity, very rarely do they provide the time and/or training to allow recruiters to be consistently successful at it. The campus recruiter--when empowered--serves as a valuable intermediary between the business and the talent market, but can only do so effectively if given the proper authority and support. This is true whether the organization is hiring 10 campus recruits or 10,000, because if entry level talent acquisition is a priority, then the organization must cultivate and support this kind of recruiting expertise.

Appropriate division of duties is another key element in building and cultivating a URR team. Like any other businesspeople, talented recruiters will actively seek out new and challenging opportunities that align with their competencies and career goals. And while creating appealing roles can be difficult with a small URR function, I've seen organizations with as few as 5-6 recruiters be very creative in this space. One of the best ways to begin this process is to assign responsibilities based on preference and skill set whenever possible. If you have a two-recruiter team, each covering 50% candidate relations and 50% recruiting operations, it may make sense to make one of them more "external" and the other "internal" facing. As the team grows, so does the number of structural options. Recruiters that see a variety of career paths are much more likely to stay with the organization ... and be more engaged on those long days on campus. Furthermore, a recruiter who feels like she/he has options is much better equipped to discuss career options with campus candidates authentically and credibly.

When organizations decide to make a more substantial investment in campus recruiting, the inevitable question becomes, "how many recruiters do I need?" Once again, there is no single right answer here, but there are some guidelines that can be used to provide direction. In my experience, I've seen ratios as low as one recruiter for every 25 recruits for specialized talent needs (like MBA or niche specialty majors), to those as high as 1:125 for disciplines that are in greater supply. As you might guess, somewhere in the middle is probably a good place to be, after taking into consideration factors like number/diversity of positions and hiring managers, geographic spread of sources, administrative and technology support, etc. Probably the best advice I can give in this regard is to find a way to make the connection between resources and results; it's a tactic employed by the most successful recruiting organizations I've been exposed to. If you can meaningfully show that having too few recruiters is *consistently* causing poorer results--low acceptance rates, poor intern conversion, higher turnover--your business case for expanding the team will get a significant boost. At EY, illustrating this correlation has allowed me to appropriately staff the recruiting team year over year because good data is very difficult to ignore.

The broader talent acquisition complement

Michael Jordan, one of the greatest basketball players of all time, once said: "talent wins games, but teamwork wins championships". This holds true in so many different aspects of life, and URR is no exception. Even the most talented recruiting team is destined to fail without help and collaboration from other parts of the organization, regardless of size, industry, or market. Finding the best way to engage, leverage, and motivate these ancillary resources is no small task given their diverse nature and the lack of direct oversight of their activities. Enlisting their help, however, can have immeasurable impact on the success of your talent acquisition efforts, so it is truly a worthwhile effort.

As the URR landscape--and the "average" campus candidate--has evolved, so has the need for more sophisticated and multi-channel efforts in the employer brand space. It is for this reason that I would prioritize branding and marketing professionals as the single most critical "non-recruiting" members of the broader URR team. Enlisting the expertise of *true* branding professionals is the key to success here; gone are the days that a recruiter with a little creativity can carry the day.

Think of your employment branding efforts as the "air strikes" that penetrate far and wide in advance of the "hand to hand combat" undertaken by the recruiting team. The more successful the former, the better your chance of success will be with the latter. In a perfect world, this would equate to fully dedicated employment brand experts focused on all aspects of talent acquisition: talent communities, social media, campus campaigns, PR, media, and internal and external communications. Realistically, you will likely need to settle for something a bit more modest, but make sure that you don't settle for too little! A couple of strategies that you can employ (pun fully intended):

- Leverage the broader consumer brand efforts in your campus recruiting campaigns, because these initiatives have a halo effect that can extend over your employer brand
- Request a partial resource or FTE from the company marketing/branding team to help with strategy and overall direction
- Engage an outside agency/consultancy for a specific campaign or content
- Hire a marketing major as an intern in the recruiting department

There are a host of other people/groups/teams that can significantly augment your URR efforts while taking pressure off the campus team itself. The largest of these is the company's own employee base. There are very few things that are more compelling or credible to a potential hire than the authentic input of a current employee of the organization. This also includes the company's alumni base that, if engaged appropriately, can share powerful, first-hand accounts of how the organization helped them grow and develop. Effectively teaming with employees and essentially re-recruiting them as brand ambassadors requires a fair amount of up-front effort, including training centered around messaging, recruiting strategy, process and procedure, and interview/evaluation skills. Many companies host "all hands" meetings at regular intervals (semi-annually, annually, etc.) to keep employees engaged and informed. These meetings can focus on recruiting for a specific line of business, geography, university, or hiring program. Employees and alumni can speak compellingly about their authentic experience within an organization, but student-to-student input is also a powerful word-of-mouth tool that can augment your recruiting efforts. That's because few sources are more credible than direct and impartial input from someone students already know and trust. Every intern headed back to campus their senior year possesses first-hand experiences with an organization that they can share with other students. And while many companies have formal campus ambassador programs that they fund and support with training, others empower these students to share their experiences with fellow students in more informal ways.

There are also a number of digital tools that can be used to maximize the relationship between the recruiting team and the business. Candidate Relationship Management software (CRM) allows for the seamless transfer of information related to candidates, campuses, events, and correspondence. Applications that allow for mass-distribution of information via employee social media accounts are readily available across multiple platforms, and video-capture technologies make creating and distributing curated content easier than ever. The bottom line is that today's employer needs to empower its full complement of staff to be de facto recruiters and ambassadors of the company brand.

A final suggestion on the broader recruiting team: seek out expertise in areas that are critical to the function. Having connections to Legal and Compliance, Risk Management, Operations/Analytics, Technology Support, and Meeting/Event Planning --to name a few--can mean the difference between a good URR effort and an outstanding one. I've seen too many great recruiters make decisions without the benefit of subject matter experts in these areas at the expense of effectiveness, efficiency or both. Look at it this way: every single person at your company was recruited in one way, shape or form; asking them to "pay it forward" by playing a part in the recruiting efforts shouldn't be too much for you to ask.

Recruiting teams of the future

Predicting the future is no easy task, but that shouldn't stop any of us from trying to anticipate and prepare for future needs. Scanning the landscape of URR, there are a few consistent themes emerging that I believe are worthy of some consideration by recruiting professionals across all industries. The first of them is that face-to-face interaction is not dead ... or dying. That's not to say that virtual interaction via video, social media and other digital touch points isn't an effective way of attracting and engaging students. These channels provide an excellent opportunity for students to explore company culture and for recruiters and candidates to meet. But the ability for a student to interact live with a company representative creates a tangible, personal connection that is very powerful. And with more and more individuals looking for careers with purpose, and companies eager to showcase their commitment to making a difference, recruiting teams that can create in-person touch points will continue to enjoy a competitive advantage. What does this mean for you? URR teams will need to be robust enough to deliver the goods.

In recent years, there have also been some interesting new evolutions in campus recruiting team structure, and I think that will continue. As the number of freelancers continues to rise in all areas of the business world, I wouldn't be surprised to see more project-based recruiting "gigs" being staffed through this medium. Similar to the contractor model, this will provide flexibility/scalability for the employer, while offering variety and work/life balance options to the freelancers. I can also envision more employers taking advantage of various insourcing/co-sourcing/outsourcing models, both for operational/administrative tasks as well as for less routine activities like employee referral intake and sourcing. Having a pool of talent that can flex to meet needs across multiple business lines, geographies, etc. will allow employers not only to meet changing needs but also provide new and different challenges to the recruiting team. Lastly, I imagine that recruiters will need to be even more globally minded and tech savvy in order to find and attract talent across multiple platforms and borders. This will "up the game" for the recruiting team of the future, requiring people with a more robust set of skills and the ability to source more creatively than in years past.

The last word

As someone who has spent over twenty years at the same (great) employer, I know that I am an anomaly in the business world. That said, there is a distinct advantage that I've enjoyed here at EY that I believe correlates to the topic of recruiting teams. I believe that success in recruiting, or any other pursuit for that matter, requires hard work, dedication, perseverance and the right environment to keep one motivated. In a people business, you are expected to bring 110% of yourself every day, and "bad days" must be kept to a minimum. For two decades, EY has found new and interesting ways to engage and challenge me, support my development, and help me upskill in a wide variety of ways. Similarly, creating a recruiting team and environment that rewards hard work and provides opportunity for URR professionals will endear them to the organization and make them true, authentic ambassadors on campus. That kind of dedication can give you an extra edge which, at the end of the day, can make all the difference.

School Selection

Bruce Soltys

School strategy. What comes to mind when you see those two little words? Are you excited by the notion of being able to refine or develop one OR are you looking for the nearest bathroom stall to hide in? Why do these two little words strike dizzying fear into so many? Throughout the next few pages, we tackle the topic head on addressing some of the most common challenges facing College Recruiting leaders tasked with creating them and offer some thoughts to help you. Ready? Good. Now unlock that bathroom stall door, head back to your desk and let's get started on crafting a leading-edge school strategy!

Step 1 - Who are you?

Just like yoga pants, one size does NOT fit all when it comes to school strategies. Has the following question been posed to you from someone a few levels above you on the org chart? "Can we take a look at what Google and Facebook are doing?" Often times it comes in the form of a statement: "Let's take a look at what Google and Facebook are doing." BREAKING NEWS - most of us do not work for Facebook and Google. Let us start with who you are developing the strategy for. Are you a large multinational fortune 1000 company? Are you a midsized regional firm? Are you a small nonprofit? What about sector? Do you identify your organization as financial services, banking, oil & gas, consulting, technology, etc.? Your answers to these questions are vital to keep in mind as we navigate through the various aspects of school strategies. What works for one company will not work for every company!

Step 2 - Where are you headed?

Ok now that we have had time to self-reflect on who we are let's talk about schools. Not so fast! Business plans these days change faster than Facebook profile pictures. That means that who you hire today may not be tasked with efforts that your company is currently engaged in. Remember 5 years ago when we were all targeting those students that could work on Big Data efforts? Yeah me neither. But, how many companies today are working on

Big Data initiatives and seeking out talent in that space? Exactly. Conversations with leadership are crucial to understand not just what skills are needed presently, but what skills sets will be the driver for the future growth of the company or organization.

There is one additional important caveat to consider during these conversations. Location, location, location. Is your company planning expansion into a new region? Are they off-shoring? Are they on-shoring? (Yes, work does come back into the U.S. sometimes)! Location is important because one of the key aspects of any school strategy should be to "do well in your backyard". In its simplest form, students attending top colleges within a pre-determined radius of your hiring locations should be well aware of the career opportunities available.

Step 3 - What are we starting with?

You know who you are. You know the skill sets you are targeting. You even know the locations of your positions. Can we please talk about schools now? Yes! Sort of. Chances are that your company already has some sort of relationships with an existing school population. They may be scattered. They may be fragmented. They may be a hot mess. The point is that they still exist. Understanding as much as you can about what the current state is an important step.

Take a quick peek out of your office or cube. See all of those people diligently working? Chances are that they graduated from college and are also doing one or more of the following – donating to their alumni association, attending sporting events back on campus, wearing their favorite collegiate logo emblazoned sweatshirt (and potentially still paying off those damn student loans). What does all this mean? It means they may have a vested interest in continuing to engage with their alumni schools and may serve as excellent company ambassadors. Determining which ones are willing (and are best suited) to act in this capacity will require more digging, but understanding the number of alumni from schools within your company is recommended.

Another key piece of insight is gathering the past hiring success from some of the pre-strategy schools. Are some schools home runs in terms of acceptance-rates? Has your company not been able to land one hire from a certain school despite numerous efforts? Once employees land in your company, how is their performance? Are employees from certain schools performing better, getting promoted faster? The answers to these will not serve up your go-forward school strategy on a platter, but it is another piece of the equation.

Dust off that copy of the org chart at the bottom of your snack drawer (we all have an emergency snack drawer at work when that case of hanger aka hunger induced anger sets in). Now take a quick peek at the names in the top levels of boxes. Chances are that those Senior Leaders also graduated from college. Their alumni donations might have a few more 000's associated with them than the employees mentioned above and they may also be serving in some sort of Board capacity at their alma mater. Should you automatically add these sets of schools to your strategy? No. Should you take them under advisement and be aware of them? Absolutely, because chances are you are going to have to defend your decision not to include some of them in your school strategy. And those are always fun times...

Step 4 – Medium data

Alumni lists. Senior leader affiliations and appointments. Hiring results. Recent hire performance indicators. You have data!! Big Data! Well, let's agree to reserve that term for financial firms, consumer insights and rocket scientists. Let us call what you now have in hand as Small Data. We are not minimizing the relevancy of it by coining it "small". Keep in mind that all of it to this point has been procured from internal channels. It is finally time to look externally. Woohoo!

Damn you Al Gore. When you created the Internet, you made it so vast. There is information everywhere!! Below are a few great resources to help you gain some additional insights:

Integrated Postsecondary Education Data System (IPEDS) - Well that certainly is a mouthful! Let us just agree to refer to it as IPEDS from here on. What is it you ask? IPEDS is a collection of annual surveys administered by the U.S National Center for Education Statistics (NECS). These surveys cover a myriad of topics including Institutional Characteristics, Institutional Prices, Student Financial Aid, Finances but most importantly for the purposes of school strategy – Enrollment Data and Degrees Conferred! Enrollment data is broken down by race/ethnicity, gender, full time/part time and undergraduate/graduate. Degrees conferred (also broken down by race/ethnicity) provide insight into the number of students who complete a postsecondary education degree by type of program. For those organizations that look to recruit individuals with niche skill sets, this is a great tool. Will the school you are looking for be represented? The good news is that the answer is "highly likely" as over 7500 institutions are represented. In fact, any college, university, technical or vocational institution that participates in the federal student financial aid programs participates. This is free to access but the data produced can be a bit raw and take some time to format.

National Association of Colleges and Employers (NACE) – To assist you with identifying the best schools that align with your recruiting targets, NACE offers School Selection Reports. Available to both members (at a discounted rate!) and non-members, they will analyze your current target schools while simultaneously offering up suggestions of new schools complete with key insights including racial and gender diversity while breaking out international students for those employers where sponsorship is not an option. This will present you with a clean data format that won't break the bank. Keep in mind that the initial data report may open up dialogue requiring additional reports down the line.

NACE Training Sessions – throughout the year, NACE offers subject matter expert led sessions focused on this exact topic! This is an instructor led delivery of rich content, case studies as well as the opportunity for deeper dialogue, questions and answers facing your organization. Check out the Events tab on the NACE site located at http://naceweb.org/events. Take a look at some of the items discussed at the most recent one held: project planning, priorities matrix, gap analysis, best practices, assessment tools, as well as selection methodologies.

Rankings – The gold standard since 1983 is US News & World Report's "Best College Rankings". Created to help parents and students make more informed decisions, many employers keep a close eye on them as well as they offer insight into several categories including National Universities, National Liberal Arts Colleges, Regional Universities & Colleges, Graduate Schools, Business Schools (or B-Schools as all the cool kids call them), Business

Programs, Engineering Programs, Law Schools, etc. While some perceive them as illustrating the quality of a particular school's academic program, others perceive them as arbitrary.

Service Providers – There are some that specialize in this space. Access to their tools would place the IPEDS data at your fingertips and offer numerous search capabilities including the option to search within a specific geographic/mileage radius and some dashboard views. While there are costs associated with their services, the annual NACE conference's vendor exposition is a great forum to meet with some of these companies and learn if their offerings fit the needs of your organization.

Consider combining some of these external data sources with the internal information that you gleaned in step 3 and now you are armed with your Medium Data.

Step 5 – Make a list and check it twice

Taking into account the workforce plans and direction of your company as well as the internal and external data sources you should now be well equipped to craft (or revise) your school list. We are not talking about a set of scribbled notes on index paper that you would take with you to the grocery store, this should be a concise well thought out view. As opposed to a numbered list of 1-25, focus on bucketing them into categories. Perhaps your Core schools are able to serve as a pipeline for all facets of your organization whereas others may fall into the niche component of Functional such as Real Estate, Actuarial or Technology. Lastly, others may serve as a Diversity pipeline and identify as HBCU (Historically Black Colleges & Universities) or HSI's (Hispanic Serving Institutions). Categories may not make sense for all, but perhaps a tiering system is more efficient (Tier 1, Tier 2, Tier 3) or Gold, Silver, Bronze. Key differentiators to define each level could focus on the following:

- Allocated budget
- Volume of on-campus activities
- Type of recruiting (on-campus vs. virtual interviewing)
- Research and development partnerships
- School team size

Keep in mind that you should be able to articulate why you chose certain schools and the data collected from the earlier steps should equip you for the conversations to come. One of the most important items to keep in mind is that if a school is NOT on your list, does not mean it is a bad school. Simply, it means that at this point it does not align as well as others do with your go-forward strategy.

Step 6 – Gain buy-in and alignment

Ok, the list is ready so print out copies and start handing them outright? Pause! We strongly recommend that the data driven list that you have created be shared with various constituents within Human Resources as well as the Business Champions within the client groups that you will be partnering with. Ask for thoughts, concerns, and candid feedback. Addressing these questions up front will offset potential derailing conversations further down the line during critical portions of the campus recruiting season when your team of recruiters and ambassadors should be making an impact on campus with students and potential applicants. As the feedback is shared with you, be sure to digest all of it and consider all recommendations while making any necessary adjustments accordingly.

Step 7 – Who are your storytellers?

No offense to anyone (myself included!) but most students only want to really talk to HR under two circumstances:

1 – You are a student studying HR and you are pursuing a career in HR
2 – When a Campus Recruiter calls you to extend an employment offer

Other than these instances, the majority of students want to interact with those working in the field/department that they are considering or with recent college hires from your company that can share their story and journey with them. This is why it is crucial to ensure you are identifying the right people to serve as ambassadors of your campus program. In addition to these campus representatives, it is imperative to work with your businesses to define the actual roles that they will play throughout the recruiting cycle and as part of the overall school teams efforts. Be sure to create clear lines of accountability as well as relevant messaging for the respective schools. Your business partners should be not only be focused on the student population but also on building relationships with the career services and faculty populations. Companies cannot spend every day on campus so equipping these key influencers with information about your opportunities will allow them to share this information with their students.

Step 8 – From strategizing to analyzing

Once your strategy is in place, you can turn your attention to analyzing it. What is working? What isn't? What are the students and faculty saying? New relationships with schools take time to build so remember to be patient. Remember that we are not flipping a switch and that one cycle is essentially one year. It may take two to three seasons to start seeing results or noticing momentum. In closing, we feel that deeper relationships with fewer schools versus surface relationships at many schools is the right approach to any successful school selection strategy. Good luck with yours!

Religion, Politics, and School Selection
Valerie Berger Fred

Introduction

I feel something like a dinosaur when it comes to campus recruiting. I have been touching the campus recruiting space in one way or another for the last 20 years. When I started, there was no technology, and intern recruitment was in the spring; now intern recruitment starts in September, nine months ahead of the internship (if not earlier than that) and there are Freshman and Sophomore programs with some firms are even doing High School outreach.

One of the first questions I am asked when people find out what I do for a living is something like, "at which schools do you recruit?" or "do you recruit at *x* school (usually their alma mater)?" While seemingly innocent, this tends to be a very loaded topic. Everyone has an opinion and everyone thinks their opinion is right. The conversation often continues with "oh, why don't you go to *y* school?" The school in reference is often one that could make great logical sense for a financial services company to recruit at and, to be honest, there often isn't a specific reason as to why we do or do not recruit at any one specific school. This tends to make these conversations difficult; especially as they are often happening in an elevator or in passing. It even occurs when I'm out socially and while I could easily spend an hour explaining our approach and the pros and cons of different schools, I have to assume I am one of the few people that would really want to have that conversation (except maybe the person reading this essay). My standard response is usually something like, "We are fortunate to live in a country with a huge number of excellent schools, but we can't recruit everywhere." Sometimes this answer is understood and we both move on; other times, more discussion follows. It is most heated when involving senior stakeholders who are vying for us to recruit at the school that they graduated from or where one of their children attends.

How many schools?

So, if you can't recruit everywhere, what is the right number? I typically suggest using several years of data and working backwards through your process starting from your ultimate hiring target. If you don't have hiring data to draw from, you would need to make some assumptions based on industry norms knowing your brand in relation to current market conditions. Remember you may be hiring interns that would convert into full time hires, so your numbers are two levels (what amount do I need next summer and what amount do I need almost two years from now). It is important to get agreement on the number of targeted schools first given the potential sensitivity in discussing the actual schools.

A simple example would be a summer intern hiring target of 30 in a process that includes an on-campus interview, final round interview and offer. To make this example more specific, let's say we are talking about a relatively well known financial services firm with good national brand recognition. Sample data is as follows - average acceptance rate (percent of offers that are accepted) is 80%, average offer rate (percent of offers extended after final rounds) is 75% and average percent of candidates progressed from on campus interview to final round interview is 50%.

In this example, you would start with 30 as your end goal and apply the percentages above which would play out as follows – Applying an 80% acceptance rate means you need to extend approximately 38 (37.5 rounded up) offers to yield your target of 30. Based on your offer rate of 75%, you would need approximately 51 (50.67 rounded up) final round candidates to yield 38 offers. Continuing to work backwards, in order to have 51 final round candidates (based on your 50% average rate of progression from on campus interview to final round interview), you would need to interview 102 candidates on campus. Most on campus interview schedules have 10-15 candidates on them. Using 12 as an average, you would need eight and one half on campus interview schedules.

Now that you have more specific and data driven guidance, you will want to consider factors specific to your firm and industry as well as school specific factors. It will vary from school to school how many schedules you can realistically rely on. For example, if you recruit at a small liberal arts college and aren't a huge brand name firm, you might struggle to fill one schedule. On the other hand, if you are recruiting at a large local university where your brand is more well-known and you might easily be able to fill two or 3 schedules. In addition to these factors, you likely will need to leave space for non-core candidates and referrals.

Taking these additional factors into consideration in the example above, it would be reasonable to recommend approximately six to eight target schools at maximum. The benefit of applying hard numbers to your recommendation is it makes it more difficult for stakeholders to argue for additional schools as it is clearly a less efficient use of resources. Once you get agreement on the number of schools, you can then begin discussions around which schools should be included. You may need to remind people of the math as conversations progress and more and more school names get thrown out for discussion.

The Fishbowl Approach

Now that the number of schools has been agreed to, it's time to figure out where you're going to recruit. When I tell people that we are fortunate to live in a country with such a wealth of excellent schools, I really do mean it. I believe that with the right recruiting processes in place, you know you could recruit anywhere and hit your target. Take all the schools, put them in a fish bowl, select your six to eight and get recruiting! Having engaged school teams and strong processes really can go a long way. That said, it is unlikely that many firms will go for the fishbowl approach.

A More Methodical Approach

If the fishbowl approach is not right for your company, there is a more methodical approach to school selection. As with the approach to determining the number of schools, some of this will depend on what kind of existing data you have. Are you building a program from scratch or refining an existing process? In either scenario, there are a few key factors that you will want to consider.

1. **Stakeholders** – Do you have buy-in from senior stakeholders who are engaged and willing to commit to travelling long distances on multiple occasions? Or should you limit your schools geographically? This could impact the size of the schools you select. As we discussed above, larger schools will likely yield more candidates (more "bang for your buck" if you will). If you only have a small team of people that you can rely on, you will want to limit the number of schools as much as possible in order to have the most impact and increase

likelihood of yield. Spreading a team too thin across more schools will likely lead to lower yield and decreased efficiency – a "lose-lose" scenario. And honestly, if the schools you choose are in line with your stakeholders' personal connections, they are more likely to participate.

2. **Location** – Your school selections should take their locations into account. Many campus programs have resources to fly all over the country, but many do not. You may need to consider the local universities as a first step as this is an economical choice and may be easier to get company representatives to go to events assuming they graduate the talent you want. If location is not an issue, your stakeholder's preference may have more weight than the location.

3. **School rank/Reputation** – While not the most important factor in my opinion, this is a factor that you will want to consider; especially, if it is something that your stakeholders are interested in knowing. There are a lot of sources for rankings, but I typically look at US News & World Report, which offers a pretty comprehensive look at a very large number of colleges and universities. Unless your stakeholders are asking for more, I think one consistent source of rankings is sufficient as a base line comparison. Which rankings you look at and how you look at them will depend on your specific program; especially if you are focused on particular areas of study like engineering or computer science.

4. **Majors or areas of specialization** - Based on your industry, you may have degree requirements for your roles or you may want to make sure that you have a diverse set of schools in the mix including Liberal Arts, Engineering and Business or Finance. If you are looking for a broad skill set, you will want to make sure your school choices reflect the same.

5. **Size of school program** - This is an important factor to consider as it will impact your likelihood of yielding candidates. Smaller programs can be good in that they may be easier to navigate and to reach your target audience and market your opportunities; however, they could be a challenge from a competition standpoint. As mentioned before, you need to be realistic about your brand and what kind of competition you might see on any campus. Larger schools may offer a greater likelihood of yield and a more diverse candidate pool, but could be more challenging to navigate.

6. **Diversity** – In an era where diversity (underrepresented minorities, women, LGBT, veterans) are highly sought after in the workforce, you should look at schools that will produce a diverse set of top talented students. There are also a number of diversity specific organizations that may allow you to target these students from your desired schools. Collaboration with these organizations does come at a cost so be prepared to pay for it if this is a priority for the organization.

Now you've picked your six to eight schools, congratulations. This can, however, be the most difficult part of recruiting. You likely needed to secure agreement from many different stakeholders in your approvals process. As you continue to go to these schools year after year, you will build a larger set of passionate alumni and will fill out your school teams. These teams, including your summer intern ambassadors (interns who have accepted full time offers to join after graduation), are key to your continued ROI at each of your schools.

Your brand is also an important element especially to the millennial generation who rely on technology to learn about firms. Be creative in how you market to this generation whether through social media, mobile friendly apps, social events that show a company's culture, and bringing back alumni to discuss the program. Having a strong brand on campus will help your ROI and acceptance yield ensuring you have chosen the correct schools, and if not, after a couple of years, do not be afraid to reassess the school list if you are not getting the results you want.

In addition to all of the factors above, if you are refining your current process, you will want to examine historical ROI from your existing efforts. It is important to keep in mind that building a brand on campus takes time and you should not rely on one season's worth of data to make decisions regarding cutting schools. That said, it is always a good idea to debrief at the end of each season; taking note of yield so that trends can be identified once you have a few season's worth of data. When considering yield, you will also want to look at intern to full time conversion numbers as well as longer term retention if that is important to your organization.

School Creep

Once you get comfortable with your agreed upon strategy and approach to target schools, it may become easy to slowly start adding new schools each year. This is something to be mindful of and may require you to go back to the original method of applying historical yields against your total number of schools to make sure your school list is not growing to the point of losing the efficiency that a campus program should offer. You may want to build this into your target collection process each year to make sure your numbers are set appropriately. If targets haven't changed and there is a compelling reason to add a new school, you will want to strongly consider cutting an existing school that has not been yielding the desired results over several seasons.

Conclusion

As technology continues to play a bigger and bigger role in the campus process, more and more firms seem to be moving to lower touch and more technology driven strategies. This may mean that a firm may have fewer true core target schools and more broad efforts at multiple schools that they are able to reach via new technologies. Research has shown that, even in their technology driven worlds, students still value a high touch, in-person process where they can meet and get to know the types of people they will be working with and get a good sense of an organization's culture. This may be the differentiating factor in why one candidate may accept your offer over a competitor's offer. In light of this, it makes sense to always have some number of core schools where you can have a higher touch, more relationship focused effort. Using the method above and considering all of the factors outlined here can assist in determining which schools those might include.

Meaningful Faculty Engagement

Laura Mills

Students are the center of attention when we visit campuses as University Relations and Recruiting (URR) professionals. As we seek to ensure the growth and productivity of our organizations, students represent talent and potential. We compete for their time and attention with passion. It's a war out there, as the title of this book suggests, and we want to win!

Look left and look right and you'll see that there are hosts of equally significant people who are also on campus with students. These are the faculty who are teaching and advising them; helping them to grow into the professionals that we want to recruit. These faculty members have dedicated their lives to preparing students to enter a multitude of professions and are key players in the campus recruiting equation.

Developing meaningful, two-way relationships with faculty is a critical component of any good URR strategy. Faculty members are influencers both in and out of the classroom. Students seek their approval from a scholarly perspective, but students also see faculty members as *in loco parentis* – Mom and Dad while at college. Today's college students study the implications of life-altering decisions from every angle and seek input from a variety of sources, including the faculty who have been teaching and guiding them throughout their academic careers. What a professor says – or doesn't say – about an industry or particular company will carry great weight in the decision-making process for today's students.

While on campus, I try to take time to speak with students who have accepted offers to work at my company, EY. In these conversations, I ask about the key drivers that drew them to EY. In most cases, students inevitably tell me that they heard about EY from a faculty member, and that conversation is often what prompted them to research EY as a potential employer. Faculty members understand that their role is to advocate for their students, not the employers seeking to recruit their students. It is, therefore, only reasonable to expect that they will also recommend our competitors. However, if EY

—

weren't top of mind and these influencers were **only** recommending our competitors, we would likely miss the opportunity to impress these bright young minds and share the value proposition of working at our organization.

In addition to guiding and advising students as they consider internship and full-time employment options after graduation, faculty and administrators can also provide your company with a competitive recruiting advantage. Faculty members know their students well and can share with you, valuable insight into how these students have performed on projects, in team-based environments and in leadership roles.

Focus your efforts

As you begin working with faculty, it is important to gain an understanding of the academic environment and how academia is structured. What are the frameworks and motivators that drive faculty? How is success measured in their eyes? As you look to integrate faculty relations as part of your overall URR strategy, consider carefully which faculty members to include in that strategy as well as who in your organization will lead the charge.

Faculty can be divided into two major camps: teaching faculty and research faculty. Teaching faculty are the "sweet spot" in any faculty relations strategy. These faculty members are those who spend time working directly with students in their classes and advising students regarding their academic and professional development, including career choice. This group of faculty are at the heart of any good faculty relationship development plan. Increasing their understanding of your profession and organization will give them knowledge that they can share with students in the classroom and as an advisor.

There is an additional distinction to be made among teaching faculty – those who teach from a textbook in a lecture-based environment versus those who teach case-based, teaming and problem-solving classes. Faculty who leverage the latter format will have significant insight into how students might perform on-the-job because they've seen students "in action."

In addition to teaching faculty members in any department, there are also faculty members who focus primarily on research. A faculty member will likely spend a great deal of time researching after they finish their PhD and first come into a tenure-track position. These younger faculty are not likely to be spending a great deal of time in the classroom working with students. Instead, these faculty members are squarely focused on their climb up the tenure ladder. Because they aren't interacting with students as much as they are researching, they aren't likely to be at the heart of your faculty relations strategy. It's important to keep them on your radar screen, however, because they will likely become accomplished and influential teachers of your target students in the future. Working with these faculty as they begin their career is a smart step towards building future good will.

There are other groups of faculty who are strong researchers. These are senior faculty members who are known for their research outcomes and related publications. Because they focus primarily on their publications, they are also not teaching a great deal. They do, however, often advise graduate students, so if graduate students are important recruiting targets, then I recommend building relationships with this group of faculty members.

Identifying which faculty are teaching versus doing research is a relatively easy task. Talk to the alumni from that school who currently work in your organization, and they can offer insight into which faculty spend time in the classroom working directly with students and which faculty are known for their research and publication outcomes.

Consider the messenger

Once you've decided to invest in building faculty relationships, you might wonder who will lead that charge on behalf of your organization. Not every URR department will have the fiscal or human resources to have a dedicated faculty relations function. But that shouldn't stop you from leveraging faculty relationships as part of your strategy to identify and attract talent. As you look at your colleagues, you're likely going to find some of them are graduates of the universities that you're targeting. These alumni are often more-than-willing to head back to campus to represent their employer, not only to students, but also to faculty members who were likely also influential in their own development. Asking alumni whom are already spending time on campus to extend their reach to include one or two of their favorite former faculty members is a great first step towards including faculty in your recruiting strategy.

No matter if it's university alumni; or a dedicated team, your faculty relations plan should be deliberate and purposeful. Once you've decided to invest in relationships with faculty, consistent outreach will show faculty that you're invested in developing deep and meaningful relationships, and that you understand and value their input and influence. Listen to faculty to learn about the key issues they are facing and seek to add value to their work so that the relationship is truly mutually beneficial.

Practical strategies

What are some tactics you can employ to build these relationships? Below, I've outlined some best practices to consider as you build a plan.

Guest lectures

The primary mission of a faculty member is to teach. Faculty members, however, and their students by the way, frequently welcome an outside perspective on course material especially from the perspective of an experienced practitioner. It's a win-win because while you're adding valuable classroom content, you're also enhancing your organization's brand.

Bringing in guest speakers with proven expertise in a given topic provides added credibility to content faculty members present. Hearing new voices provides students not only with different points of view, but also with potential resources they can apply in later courses and rely on when making career choices. Your practitioners can add value to the curriculum and provide students with first-hand insight into the work that they have an interest in pursuing.

Once you've been invited into a class, it's important to make a strong positive impression. Your practitioners are a representative of your company's brand, as well as their own personal brands. Leveraging interactive teaching techniques like case studies and group projects will keep students engaged and increase your odds of a repeat invitation to present in that class.

Faculty often serve as advisors to student clubs and organizations, and working with these faculty members to provide content and resources to student groups is another avenue to consider as part of your faculty relations efforts. The time your practitioners spend presenting to student clubs and organizations will not only enhance your organization's brand, but will also give you an opportunity to interact with students and see their ability to grasp content and assert their leadership skills. In essence, you'll have the opportunity to get a sneak-peak at great talent and perhaps pre-identify some terrific recruits.

Professional associations

Joining and maintaining active membership in academic professional associations is a strong signal that your company is committed to working with faculty. Professional associations are always in need of program ideas, talented presenters, and individuals who can organize and produce programs. Membership in an academic professional association is a great way to extend the reach of your brand message while contributing valuable skills to the association.

If active participation in a professional association is daunting, consider sponsorship as a means to becoming involved. Sponsoring is a less time-intensive way to participate but especially important to associations and their budgets. When you provide financial or logistical support to the association you receive significant brand exposure and plenty of member goodwill. No matter the path that you choose, the ability and opportunities to network through academic professional associations is a valuable way to expand relationship with faculty and raise the profile of your company's brand.

Thought leadership

Faculty are passionate about sharing knowledge. Your company likely shares publications and thought leadership with clients and customers on a regular basis, and you should consider sharing those resources with faculty as well. They'll appreciate this fresh source of content and may even consider sharing it with students if it's relevant to what they're talking about in class. Whether you send hardcopies with a short note to individual faculty members, or broadcast digital versions via electronic newsletters to an organized distribution list, thought leadership provides relevant knowledge to faculty while keeping your brand top-of-mind.

Don't limit your sharing of information to publications. Faculty are often looking to maintain professional licensure, and inviting them to CPE-bearing webinars and trainings will give them insight into leading-edge issues that you have in common and will also support them in keeping their credentials current.

Advisory boards

Faculty and administrators at colleges and universities are interested in partnering with stakeholders to increase the relevance and quality of their academic programs. Advisory boards can support this by providing guidance and feedback. Being invited to sit on a school or university-wide advisory board will provide invaluable exposure to faculty and academic leadership.

As an advisory board member, you'll help ensure that a school's program is current and aligned to current business practices. You'll have the opportunity to benefit from the mutual exchange of ideas between industry representatives and faculty and will be called upon to advise and assist faculty regarding program promotion, curriculum innovation, job placement, and evaluation.

Final thoughts

It is vital to listen and learn when working with faculty. Communication goes two ways and you have as much to learn from faculty members as they do from you. Academics welcome input from practitioners and the insight that faculty have to share regarding their college and students will help give your organization a competitive advantage as your seek out the best and brightest talent.

As you broaden your outreach efforts while on campus to include work with faculty, you're sure to feel the impact on your recruiting results.

The Why and the How: New Perspectives on Diversity Recruiting

Adrienne Alberts and Ayanna Wilcher

Acquiring the best and brightest talent is an essential endeavor for organizations. The unique characteristics of university and diversity recruiting add to the intricacies of effectively acquiring talent; but unlike traditional recruiting that thrives on acquiring talent quickly, university and diversity recruiting require an investment of time to build relationships with targeted communities. It is a competency whose mastery lives somewhere between art and science, ultimately a balance of both. As recruitment professionals, it is critical that we excel in the art and science of recruitment;–it is important to remain abreast of what is happening in the industry and to periodically remind ourselves why it is important to engage in this work. As you read this essay, we will first elevate your understanding of the foundations of diversity recruiting and provide a contemporary business case for these recruiting efforts. We will then explore shifts in the diversity landscape and finally introduce a new way of examining the success of your efforts.

The business case for diversity recruiting

The most important and compelling reasons to invest in a university based diversity program–reach back to the 1960's and originate in compliance and affirmative action. At that time, the prevailing line of thinking centered on building diversity throughout an organization by recruiting exceptional talent from universities, retaining them and promoting from within.

Over time as business needs and population demographics shifted, alternate benefits for building a diverse workforce began to emerge which included the clear moral imperative; it was simply the right thing to do. However, in order to build consistent support for diversity recruiting initiatives, strong moral imperative aside; programs would need to positively impact the bottom line. Whether in a for-profit or non-profit, the bottom line is critical to an institution's ability to live out its mission.

Today, research clearly articulates the benefits of diversity recruiting programs, building a contemporary business case. Marcus Robinson, Charles Pfeiffer and Joan Buccigrossi (2003) highlighted an alternative benefit:

Organizations that are successful in leveraging the diversity of their people are better able to adapt to changes in the external environment. They are more innovative in anticipating and responding to these changes

In that same research, authors pointed to the work of Harvard researcher, John Kotter (as cited in Robinson et al, 2003), who showed that:

So called "adaptive cultures" dramatically outperformed "non-adaptive" cultures across a variety of factors.

Those factors included increased revenues, expanded workforce, increased stock price/market valuation, and improved net incomes. With those factors alone it would be compelling for organizations to invest in building and promoting diversity and inclusion, but those aren't the only benefits. Engagement of employees has also been highlighted as a benefit of a diverse workforce in research.

In the Corporate Executive Board White Paper on "Creating Competitive Advantage Through Workforce Diversity," (2012) it was reported that:

The bottom line, though, is that diversity is good for business. CEB research found that in a more diverse and inclusive workforce, individual discretionary effort improves by 12% and intent to stay improves by 20%. Team collaboration and commitment improve by approximately 50%. In short, working in an organization environment where divergent perspectives are valued makes employees want to work harder, stay longer, and be stronger team players. The numbers tell us that diversity and inclusion aren't just theoretically important, morally important, and legally important. Diverse and inclusive workforces drive outcomes that are important to the business.

As we look at specific programs that touch the university space, there continues to be value in the stream of thought that building from within is effective. Reasons for investing in diversity recruiting continue to expand, and an even more compelling reason has also emerged. With the extreme pace of change in business, the ongoing influence of technology and the changes in population demographics, universities provide a source of talent with innate knowledge of these conditions. These students have grown up expecting things to change quickly driven by advancements in-technology and they are intimately familiar with exceling in that environment. It is their everyday reality. Their ability to understand and natively engage in these environments creates an advantage.

Finally, organizations are increasingly being required to share diversity demographics and recruitment data when bidding for business and as a part of sales proposals. Requests for diversity demographics of organizational workforces are also being audited by organizations utilizing a company's services. With increasing scrutiny on organizational demographics, it is important for organizations to remain steadfast in their commitment to recruit the most diverse and effective workforce.

The business case for diversity is clear, but this article is intended to shake up your thinking, encourage you to find new ways to engage, and also warn you to look around as the landscape has and will continue to change!

Some things have changed - new diversities are heading your way

We have moved well beyond ethnicity and gender as the core demographics when speaking about diversity. With the changing student demographics and characteristics of recent generations, there are shifts we must have on our radar. The world is no longer black and white and as leaders we find ourselves faced with new issues for the changing workforce. Below are three issues regarding sexual orientation, individuals with disabilities and ethnic identities that add an additional challenge in diversity recruiting.

In 2012 and 2015, the Equal Employment Opportunity Commission (EEOC) appealed and won decisions that upheld sexual orientation and gender identity as protected classes (US Equal Employment Opportunity Commission, 2015). Previously there were prevailing social justice constructs that encouraged organizations to be inclusive, but the legal standing as a protected class was unclear. With the EEOC appeals, this is no longer a question. Furthermore, additional areas of gender identify and sexual orientation have begun to merge including Intersexuality, Asexuality, and Pansexuality each challenging our traditional approaches of connecting with these communities.

Beyond gender identity and sexual orientation, students with disabilities are enrolling in institutions of higher education at an increasing rate with the largest increase being students with "hidden disabilities," including learning disabilities or psychiatric disorders (Mercer, 2012). The Office of Federal Contractor Compliance Programs added new rules to improve the employment of individuals with disabilities by developing specific hiring goals. These trends create opportunities and challenges for employers, as today's students are much less likely to identify themselves as diverse or to disclose a disability.

With increasing frequency, students from targeted diverse populations are rejecting the use of conventional characteristics to define themselves. Opting not to count themselves among certain diverse categories nor to disclose a disability. Though students may not align themselves with diverse characteristics, they do understand the value of equality, access, and have an appreciation for what makes each individual unique. They embrace the core tenants of inclusion and are looking to work for organizations that can demonstrate that they understand and promote the same values.

With all of these variables, it is important to remain abreast of ongoing changes on the diversity landscape but it is equally important to make sure you understand how your organization defines diversity so that you can direct your efforts to yield the expected results.

Your proven approach should remain consistent

Now that we understand the landscape and have explored what diversity means to our organizations we must intentionally consider the implications for our recruiting approaches. Since the foundation of relational recruiting is building solid relationships, let's start there.

Build relationships

If you think about identifying diverse candidates in the same way that we think about other passive candidates it sheds new light on the process. Doing research to understand where to find the candidates you seek is the starting point. It is difficult to find individuals if you don't know where to look. The NACE School Selection report is a great resource to use to understand the diversity demographics for a campus and within a major. Using that data to narrow your institutional focus will allow you to effectively aim recruitment resources at the fundamental work of building substantive relationships.

It is important to note that your diversity target schools may differ from your core schools. While you may target specific schools because of their diversity profiles, there are ways to find diverse talent within your core schools as well by leveraging relationships.

In order to maximize candidate attraction, networking and building relationships with the organizations that cater to diverse individuals is a must. Surface activities are not enough. For example, it isn't enough to host a Welcome Back table in the university center and expect that you are going to attract top diverse candidates. You have to be strategic and find out where students are and what organizations exist on campus. Building relationships with and through career centers is key to your recruiting strategy but don't stop there. When it comes to diversity recruiting you need to add a few new allies to your list. In addition to your current campus partners, consider adding disability services, faculty and administrators who advise student organizations, campus leaders focused on pride programming, and the campus chief diversity officer. It is important to be knowledgeable when you engage students with the ability to relate to their experience and these new campus allies are indispensable in that regard. They have the pulse on the diverse student population and can provide insight on relevant issues and the current campus climate. They are your key to identifying non-traditional events to participate in, connecting with student leaders directly, and bridging the gap as student leaders transition from year to year.

Select the best recruiting team

We are beginning to see members of Generation Z in our recruitment events. Generation Z was born in 1996 and they are the last generation that will be over 50% Caucasian (Peterson, 2016). Although this generation doesn't want to be singled out for the diverse group they represent they do want to feel represented by individuals in your organizations throughout the recruiting process. Be mindful of the professionals you have involved. Did you bring all non-diverse professionals to a National Society of Black Engineers event? During the office visit did they see other diverse professionals? Did you create an environment in which they could picture themselves thriving in the

---

future? It's important to get your employee networks involved to assist with the recruiting process. Diverse business resource groups and alumni from targeted schools are exceptional allies in the recruiting process, from prescreening, to campus events, the interview process and even the offer process.

Focusing on the perception of the recruiting team and working environment isn't enough to seal the deal. Having everyone participating in the recruitment process trained to identify diverse talent is equally important. It is essential that-recruiters are trained to screen in candidates with the potential to enhance diversity within your organization and interviewers are trained to understand and respect differences without bias.

When reviewing candidate resumes think about how the candidate can enhance diversity within your organization. Check to see what school they attend and what clubs or organizations they've been involved with. Are they from an HBCU? Do they belong to a veterans group, a Latino student association or a member of a historically black fraternity or sorority? Have they participated in the Emerging Leaders internship program designed to provide students with disabilities an opportunity to compete for highly competitive internships? Looking for opportunities to bring students with these types of experiences into your candidate pool increases your chances to build diversity.

Ensure that interviewers participate in cultural competence and unbiased interviewing training. We all have biases that impact our interactions. It is important to identify these biases before tripping over them in the interview process and working through tactics to minimize their impact on your organizations recruiting effort.

Reflect your commitment in your marketing materials

Be mindful of the marketing materials and collateral that you are using on campus. Incorporate diversity into your employment brand. Does your brand reflect the diversity you are striving to obtain? It's important to have marketing materials that consistently reflect diversity especially when you are at diverse events. But beyond diversity recruiting events, it should be visible in all employment branding collateral so candidates see consistency and a commitment to diversity throughout your brand. In many cases, diverse candidates know that employers are competing for them. Reflecting diversity as a core component of your employment brand can help close the deal.

Measure success quantitatively and qualitatively

Measuring diversity recruiting efforts is as important as executing them. Taking stock in program performance provides opportunities to celebrate success and invest in continuous improvement. Before stepping on campus, define key metrics to evaluate recruiting performance. Select repeatable measures designed to show progress towards your goal and follow candidates through the recruitment funnel: the percentage of diverse individuals in resume submissions, interviews, offers, and hires for internships and full-time. This approach can provide insights into individual school performance and can show trends year over year.

But traditional performance indicators aren't enough as they often fall short of measuring the full efficacy of diversity programs. Measuring hires, promotion rates, and rakings on the best places to work lists tell a part of the story, but the true measure of the maturity of a program is how it is woven into the fabric of an organization. The most mature diversity recruitment programs become an institutional imperative where values and actions align and are embraced as a common responsibility shared by all. When an organization has a mature diversity recruiting program, organizational leaders care about diversity and inclusion efforts and review key metrics along with other measures of overall organizational success. They speak about diversity as an organizational imperative. Managers not only embrace differing perspectives and approaches in their teams, they seek them out. Employees are actively involved in diversity recruiting efforts whether through involvement in a business resource group or as an ambassador sharing relevant openings throughout their networks via social media. Everyone has a part to play and they play it willingly.

This is an idealistic view of diversity recruiting within an organization, so it is important to point out that maturity exists on a continuum and organizations will be at different places along that continuum. For example, an organization may have low cultural competence but a sincere belief that diversity recruitment is everyone's responsibility; or vice versa, employees with high cultural competence may have little regard for the need to integrate efforts at every level of the organization.

Using a maturity measure in addition to traditional metrics can provide a thorough understanding of your efforts. To assess your programs maturity, ask yourself a few key questions:

- Who is responsible for diversity recruiting in your organization? Is it the responsibility of one team or department, or is it there a collective responsibility?
- How do organizational leaders participate in and speak about diversity recruiting and workforce inclusion efforts?
- Are managers culturally competent? Are they aware of their biases and impact they can have on the recruitment process?
- Are recruiters finding ways to screen diverse candidates in rather than out?
- Is training available for all individuals who support diversity recruiting efforts? Is that training required?

As you answer these questions, assess your program and identify opportunities for change. This essay is intended to be a tool to help you diagnose if your diversity recruiting strategy remains relevant today in four accessible and actionable steps. First, use the contemporary business case to expand the way you speak about the importance of diversity recruiting with internal stakeholders and organizational leaders. Second, utilize the trending information to examine your organization's approach to diversity and if it is inclusive of emerging populations. Third, assess if your programmatic approach is dependent on populations willingness to self-identify or does it integrate the message of diversity so seamlessly that everyone will understand your commitment. Fourth, allow the maturity model to help you prioritize where to begin.

Finally, and perhaps the most significant, in your assessment of the current state, it is important not to lose sight of what may be on the horizon. It isn't enough to make changes to meet today's challenges. Things will continue to evolve and your program's success will require continuous development.

Remember the most mature recruitment programs will fuel an organization's capability to adapt and lead into the future. The real question is: Will your organization be among them?

References:

Corporate Executive Board. (2012). *Creating Competitive Advantage Through Workforce Diversity Seven Imperatives and Inventive Ideas for Companies That Want to Get It Right.* Corporate Executive Board Company.

Marcus Robinson, C. P. (2003). *Business Case for Diversity with Inclusion.* Rochester: wetWare, Inc. Retrieved from Workforce Diversity Network.

Marcus Robinson, C. P. (2003). *Business Case for Diversity with Inclusion.* Rochester: wetWare, Inc.

Mercer, K. A. (2012). *Students with Learning Disabilities and Attention Disorders: Stories of the College Choice Process.* North Carolina State University, Higher Education Administration. Raleigh: Kerri A. Mercer.

Peterson, S. (2016, January 12). Strategy and Growth Consultant. *Diversity And Inclusion In The Workplace.* San Francisco, California, U.S.: AfterCollege.

US Equal Employment Opportunity Commission. (2015, January 25). *Federal Agencies: Other Federal Protections.* Retrieved from U.S. Equal Employment Opportunity Commission Website: http://www.eeoc.gov/federal/otherprotections.cfm

Recruiting Candidates with Disabilities

Janine Rowe and Alan Muir

In recent years, recruiters have turned their attention on individuals with disabilities in part to support diversity and inclusion recruitment goals, but also to satisfy new Section 503 standards for federal contractors requiring a 7% workforce utilization goal for employees with disabilities. In order to successfully recruit candidates with disabilities, employers should understand the current climate for individuals with disabilities in higher education and employment, and develop specific recruiting strategies to reduce barriers in reaching this population.

The current state of disability, higher education, and employment in the U.S.

The number of individuals in the United States with disabilities, currently the largest minority population at approximately 50 million, is expected to continue to grow (Brault, 2012). Due to Section 504 of the Rehabilitation Act of 1973 and Americans with Disabilities Act (ADA) of 1990, individuals with disabilities are attending college in greater numbers than ever before. Students with disabilities represent 11.1% of the general college student population, equating to about 1.5 million students (National Center on Education Statistics, 2016). While federal laws have increased individuals with disabilities' access to higher education, students who choose this path still face challenges and may need greater support during the transition from high school. As compared to their peers without disabilities, students with disabilities have lower retention and persistence rates, and take more time to complete their degrees (Wessel, Jones, Markle, & Westfall, 2009).

College campuses represent a diverse landscape of various types of disabilities. Approximately 70% of college students with disabilities have non-apparent disabilities, or disabilities not necessarily visible to others (including learning disabilities, psychiatric disabilities, and chronic health conditions). Currently, learning disabilities represent the most prevalent type of disability on college campuses, followed by chronic health conditions, psychiatric disabilities, speech or language disabilities, vision loss (blindness and low vision), hearing loss (deaf and hard of hearing), Autism Spectrum Disorders, and traumatic brain injuries (National Center for Education Statistics, 2016). The number of students with psychiatric disabilities has rapidly increased over the past several years, and is expected to grow as schools report large increases in the prevalence of students with mental health concerns (Gruttadaro & Crudo, 2012). Currently, 24% of college students report at least one mental health disorder (National Center on Education Statistics, 2009).

Disability Student Services (DSS) Offices on campuses have grown to meet the needs of this expanding population. Under the ADA and Section 504, higher education institutions must provide equal access to education. Therefore, academic accommodations are a critical tool in facilitating student success. Many students will use instructional or testing accommodations to support their academic progress, often replicating accommodations used in high school settings. While the accommodations may be similar for students, the process for requesting accommodations is separate and distinct in each educational setting. In the K-12 setting, students in need of accommodations are identified by teachers and administrators, and accommodations are selected by the students' IEP team, with little, if any, input from the student ("Protecting our students with disabilities," 2015).

Self-efficacy and self-advocacy are required for college students with disabilities to navigate the accommodations request process. The student is responsible for initiating and completing a multi-step process, including visiting the DSS office on campus, providing written documentation of their disabilities from a medical or similar professional, working with disability service offices to determine appropriate accommodations, and communicating with faculty about use of their accommodations. The most frequent accommodations provided are alternate exam formats or additional exam time, followed by tutors to assist with coursework, readers or classroom note-takers, academic support such as tutoring, alternative exam formats, and adaptive equipment or technology (Raue & Lewis, 2011).

Not all students who register with their campus' DSS Office will receive accommodations. Accommodations are only granted to students whose functional limitations indicate a need for an educational accommodation (Herbert, et. al. 2014). In many cases, however, accommodations are crucial to students' success. Use of academic accommodations is found to have a significant positive impact on students' GPA. Use of test accommodations (such as time extension and modification of materials) and course accommodation (such as assignment accommodation) showed the most significant influence on GPA (Kim & Lee, 2015).

College students with disabilities who persist to earn a degree and enter the workforce may still experience challenges: while unemployment for people with disabilities had decreased steadily in recent years, employment for college graduates with disabilities still lags behind that of college graduates without disabilities. A survey of over 400 graduates with disabilities confirmed an unemployment rate among college graduates with disabilities of 46%. They are highly likely to be underemployed: among respondents who were working, 52.4% were working full time and 35.8% of those working were making less than $10,000 per year (Maduas & Gelbar, 2013). Those who attain employment will find the disclosure process similar to what they experienced in college: they have the choice to disclose their disability to their employer, decide whom they wish to tell and at which point during the job search process, and select accommodations to request. Not every graduate who has requested accommodations from their campus DSS will disclose to their employers: approximately 66% of graduates disclosed the presence of a disability, primarily to their supervisor, and 50.3% of the time, the disclosure was to request a workplace accommodation (Maduas & Gelbar, 2013).

Previous negative experiences are often cited as reasons for college graduates not to disclose their disability: 43.4% of graduates reported that they experienced negative effects after disclosing, including negative judgments made about their ability to successfully perform in the job and felt stigma associated with the disability (Madaus and Gelbar, 2013). Factors that increased the likelihood of disclosing to an employer include having a disability that requires an accommodation, having an open and accepting relationship with a supervisor, and perception of their employer as "disability-friendly (von Schrader, Malzer, Erickson, & Bruyere, 2011).

Why should recruiters target college students with disabilities?

Employers have been seeking diversity in their workforces for many years. Until recently, diversity recruiting focused on the more historically traditional areas of race, gender and ethnicity. In the U. S. alone, there are 57 million people with self-identified disabilities, solidifying this group as the largest minority group and representing about 20 percent of the national population (Donovan, 2012). Individuals with disabilities are economically influential: the aggregate discretionary spending power of this group is $220 billion. In 2006, the American Association of People with Disabilities (AAPD) commissioned a survey conducted by Public Opinion Research Inc. that found "more than 70% of the association's members choose to shop with retailers that demonstrate their support for people with disabilities ("Why Target People with Disabilities?", 2015)." This indicates a preference in the market toward businesses and corporations that employ persons with disabilities as well.

This economic incentive and the Americans with Disabilities Act of 1990 (ADA) have been present for a number of years, yet the pace of hiring persons with disabilities has not increased. In 2013, the U. S. Department of Labor's Office of Federal Contract Compliance Programs (OFCCP) announced changes to Section 503 of the Rehabilitation Act of 1973. This Section of the Act focused on increasing the employment of people with disabilities and creating measures of success for disability hiring. Employers covered by the requirements are private sector corporations or non-profit organizations that have more than $50,000 in annual contracts with any portion of the Federal government and OFCCP estimates the number of organizations subject to this regulation is between 250,000 and 300,000.

The 2014 changes included a 7% aspirational goal of disability representation in specific job categories of these organizations, however, employers have had difficulty accurately tracking and counting the number of employees or potential candidates in the pipeline that have a disability. OFCCP received legal approval to devise a requirement for Section 503 employers to "invite" all current employees and candidates to disclose the presence of a disability without providing further details, documentation or requesting an accommodation. All candidates are invited in the early pre-offer stages and again after the job offer, through a standardized one-page Self-ID form that simply asks if the respondent has a disability and they can answer "Yes," "No" or "I Prefer Not to Answer." The Self-ID form is to only be used as a data collection tool for the employer to know where the candidate with a disability is in the applicant tracking system and whether that candidate was hired by the company. The signature is required to allow the company to properly count the number of persons with disabilities applying for that specific job category or currently employed in that category. For current employees, employers are required to survey all employees with the Self-ID form at a minimum of once every five years, similar to what is done to gather veteran information. All information gathered from the Self-ID forms are compiled and aggregated for reporting to OFCCP on a regular basis and in an annual report in the same way as all other affirmative action reporting.

Since the implementation of the changes to the regulation, employers have been faced with the uncertainty of the accuracy of the count of candidates or employees with disabilities within their companies. Employers must educate candidates or current employees that the completion of the Self-ID form has no bearing on the hiring results or other future personnel decisions made about a current employee. Initially, employees may see little direct benefit to affirmatively answering the question, however, it is incumbent upon the employer to provide a corporate culture that is welcoming and inclusive of diversity of all types, including disability. The long-term benefit to every person with a disability, who is seeking to be hired by these companies that a truthful, affirmative answer on that form sends a message to the company that there is a benefit to outreaching to diverse populations and being aggressive in recruiting the best talent available. It will also, over time, help to codify the inclusive culture being instituted by the employer, making it easier for future employees and candidates to know that they can disclose on the Self-ID form and understand that there will be no repercussions for self-identifying, but in fact it will provide role models for others to follow and increase the overall diversity of the company.

Another major challenge with Section 503 is that since higher education was not specifically included in the discussion of the changes to the regulation, there remains significant confusion among higher education professionals, who counsel students with disabilities about career preparation and the issues of disclosure. In turn, students and recent graduates with disabilities are not aware or are confused to the point of feeling compelled to fully disclose their disability when presented with a Self-ID form, and to submit potentially sensitive documentation. Higher education and students with disabilities need to be made aware of the distinction between the invitation to Self-ID under Section 503 and the opportunity to voluntarily self-disclose with documentation to support a workplace accommodation request as prescribed under the ADA.

How should recruiters target individuals with disabilities?

Recruiters naturally look to college campuses to meet their disability recruiting goals, but often have difficulty finding access to students with disabilities. Often, the professionals who work most closely with students with disabilities are in DSS Offices and may not have a strong connection to Career Services Offices or campus recruiting partners. This creates a gap between job-seeking students with disabilities and employers who are committed to hiring individuals with disabilities.

Suggested strategies to close the gap include increasing support the collaboration between Career Services and DSS offices, increasing visibility on college campuses, leveraging employee resource groups (ERG's), and providing training to managers and co-workers. In planning a recruiting strategy, particularly under the mandate of the changes to Section 503, the most successful option is to continue to focus on the company's target schools. Successful companies use the influence and the relationships they have developed over a period of time to request the Career Services contact to have the slate of candidates include students with disabilities. If the Career Services representative is hesitant about how to accomplish this, ask if the office has a collaborative relationship with DSS. If there is no such relationship, the company should encourage the development of that relationship and request to meet with the DSS director to express the company's interest in meeting students with disabilities. If that still does not work, then suggest a resource such as Career Opportunities for Students with Disabilities (COSD) that will assist the university Career Services office in developing that relationship and help to explain the importance of the employer meeting the requirements under the current Section 503.

There are a number of higher education best practices that promote the collaboration required for a company to successfully recruit students with disabilities. One example is at Rochester Institute of Technology (RIT) and the National Technical Institute for the Deaf, one of RIT's nine colleges for Deaf and hard-of-hearing students. RIT has done an exemplary job of aligning the needs of students with disabilities represented by their DSS office, NTID and the Spectrum Support Program to be referred to Career

Services and are available to recruiters seeking these students. This collaboration promotes clear communication among several offices at RIT, and makes use of a voluntary release form offered to students in the DSS Office, which gives permission for DSS to share students' names with Career Services. This allows Career Services to provide information about disability-recruiting events and job openings directly to students with disabilities. An appointed liaison working from each office can help employers coordinate recruitment efforts and directly connect students and employers appropriately.

Another higher education best practice that can be highlighted is Northeastern University's "Wraparound Model" that includes DSS, Career Services and the Co-Operative Education office to provide seamless service to students with disabilities. Northeastern has the requirement of a co-op in nearly all of its academic majors and having all of the offices collaborating to assist in having students with disabilities available for recruitment and selection for co-op experiences and ensure that the proper workplace accommodations are in place. A major component of this Wraparound Model is the Employer in Residence program that invites employer representatives to be in the DSS office a few hours a week to meet with DSS staff and students. This program takes away the uneasiness students feel when interacting with employers, as the staff gains trust in the commitment of employers to hire students with disabilities and encourages students to make appointments with the employer representative for mock interviews, networking, or to conduct an informational interview. This is a unique and effective tool and helps Northeastern to exhibit a high level of expertise that employers seek in their higher education relationships, as they grapple with the mandate of Section 503.

Being highly transparent in promoting the diversity values of companies and include disability in those values have shown a greater benefit. Emphasizing "Disability Inclusive Diversity" in advertising, branding and website presence has a profound effect, as today's students are the most media-savvy generation and take their cues from what they see in various forms of promotion. EY, Nordstrom and Microsoft are examples of emphasizing the use of models with apparent disabilities in their advertising. Verizon showcases stories of their employees with disabilities inside and outside of the company.

Employers can also leverage traditional diversity recruiting events such as meet-and-greet sessions or affinity receptions by specifically inviting student disability-advocacy organizations. Employers can also increase their visibility among students with disabilities by sending employees with disabilities to recruit on college campuses and incorporating examples of disability-inclusive culture in company presentations, in company literature (web and print), and on social media.

Many successful companies that recruit college graduates with disabilities have active Employee Resource Groups (ERGs) that focus on disability. For many years, companies have been eager to create ERGs for the primary diversity populations including women, African-Americans, Latinos and LGBT. More recently, employers have been active in creating ERGs for those employees with disabilities. For example, AT&T and Delta Air Lines have exemplary disability ERGs that not only are opportunities for employees with disabilities to feel a sense of belonging or camaraderie with other employees with disabilities, but have actually been integral in the development of products, test-marketing ideas or making significant changes in the management practices of these companies. For example, AT&T's IDEAL group was originally made up of regional groups that were formed when AT&T was broken up into the "Baby Bells." Those groups then were united under the IDEAL banner when AT&T absorbed all of the regional communications companies to make up the current day AT&T. With this history, there is a greater diversity of thought from the various regions that has benefitted the larger company. IDEAL has participated in focus groups about accessibility of mobile technologies and the creation of new practices that concentrate on capturing the disability market. Delta Air Lines' ABLE group has grown significantly in 2015 alone from just under 400 members to now more than 625 members. ABLE, in conjunction with an external advisory group, the Advisory Board on Disability (ABD), has shaped how Delta improves its customer service to travelers with disabilities. The ABD is comprised of prominent and successful people with disabilities representing government, non-profits and corporations, who are loyal customers of the airline and are eager to provide insights into the travel experience of a person with a disability. Companies with disability ERGs can send employees from the group on recruiting trips and should mention the presence of the ERG in promotional materials.

Disability-related training is a critical step in preparing an organization to recruit, hire, retain and promote individuals with disabilities. Employers are not required to provide training to their employees under the ADA, however, it is crucial to provide education and support to managers and co-workers who will be working most closely with employees with disabilities. Training helps support an inclusive corporate culture by reducing stereotyping and unconscious biases, and address misconceptions about employees with disabilities (such as viewing a reasonable accommodation as an unfair advantage or assuming that providing accommodations is expensive or time-consuming). Potential training tasks include: Disability employment laws, processes for requesting and providing reasonable accommodations, disability etiquette, and interviewing candidates with disabilities. Training materials, including articles and webinars, are readily available via AskJan.org and Office of Disability Employment Policy (ODEP).

Many employers choose to create an online resource center for employees to access the materials as needed. Some employers choose to work with community partners, such as local disability advocacy groups or vocational rehabilitation centers. Employers will also find valuable information from networking with other employers who have strong disability recruiting programs. US Business Leadership Network (USBLN) supports disability hiring through networking opportunities and education with affiliates in nearly every state. Career Opportunities for Students with Disabilities (COSD) also supports employers by disseminating information about best practices in disability hiring, hosting a web portal for employers to advertise job openings to students with disabilities, and providing networking opportunities at their national conference. Employers can also call upon their disability ERGs for information about best practices in managing and supervising employees with disabilities.

To reach qualified candidates with disabilities, companies should leverage campus relationships, increase visibility with targeted student groups, and take advantage of resources like disability ERGs and training materials. These strategies will help companies reach two goals: successfully integrating employees with disabilities into their corporate cultures and satisfy Section 503 disability hiring requirements.

References:

Brault, M. (2012). Americans with disabilities: 2010. United States. Bureau of the Census.

Donovan, R. (2012). Emerging Giant – Big is not big enough, the global economics of disability. Retrieved from: https://www.essentialaccessibility.com/

Gruttadaro. D., & Crudo, D. (2012). College students speak: A survey report on mental health. National Alliance on Mental Illness (NAMI). Fairfax, VA.

Herbert, J.T., Welsh, W., Hong, B.S., Soo-yong, B., Atkinson, H.A., & Anne Kurz, C. (2014). Persistence and Graduation of College Students Seeking Disability Support Services. Journal of Rehabilitation, 80(1), 22-32.

Kim, W. H., Lee., J. (2015). The effect of accommodation on academic performance of college students with disabilities. *Rehabilitation Counseling Bulletin.* Vol. 1, n 11. Pp. 1-11.

Madaus, J., & Gelbert, N. (2013). Disability and Stigma. Unpublished manuscript.

National Center on Education Statistics. (2009). 1999-2000 National Postsecondary Aid Study. Washington, DC: U.S. Department of Education.

U.S. Department of Education, National Center for Education Statistics. (2016). Digest of Education Statistics, 2015 (NCES 2016-014).

National Council on Disability. (2000). National Disability Policy: A progress report. Washington DC: Author.

Raue, K., and Lewis, L. (2011). Students with disabilities at degree-granting postsecondary institutions (NCES 2011–018). U.S. Department of Education, National Center for Education Statistics. Washington, DC: U.S. Government Printing Office.

Protecting Students with Disabilities. (2015). Retrieved from http://www2.ed.gov/about/offices/list/ocr/504faq.html

von Schrader, S., Malzer, V., Erickson, W, and Bruyere, S. (2011). Emerging Employment Issues for People with Disabilities: Disability disclosure, leave as reasonable accommodation, use of job applicant screeners. Report of a Cornell/AAPD Study. Ithaca, NY: Cornell University Employment and Disability Institute.

Wessel, R.D., Jones, J.A., Markle, L., and Westfall, C. (2009). Retention and Graduation of Students with Disabilities: Facilitating student success. Journal of Postsecondary Education and Disability, Vol 21, N3, p116-125.

Why target people with disabilities? (2015). Retrieved from: http://www.realeconomicimpact.org/asset-development-community/the-business-case

Developing Critical Sales Skills: Recruiting for Success

Helen Brown

In 2017, up to 35% of the total workforce will be entrepreneurial, according to Fast Company (Dishman, 2017). This exhibits an undeniable shift in a portion of the labor market called the gig economy which consists primarily of short-term engagements and temporary positions.

There are two types of entrepreneurship: the good kind where people see a need and a way to make money from that need, and therefore start a company. And then there's the bad kind. These people start businesses because they can't find employment elsewhere (Buchanan, 2017. If students will be peaking in the age of entrepreneurship, they will need to learn soft skills to form a strong foundation for themselves as professionals in the gig economy.

The CEO of RiseSmart, Sanjay Sathe, said: "Where freelancing was most often thought of for creative work and contracting was thought of for IT-related positions, the gig economy has begun to encompass all types of roles" (Dishman, 2017). Similarly, the CEO of Mosquito Joe, Kevin Wilson, stated, "We can find strong younger people who have good technical skills, but they are also required to deal with franchisees, who may get nervous or upset about something. The younger people often have not developed the skills to handle that. But [older applicants] may not have the technical skills to keep up with our pace. We ultimately find candidates who satisfy both requirements; it just takes time" (Buchanan, 2017).

Because of this change in roles, it is imperative for companies to focus efforts on sharpening their employees' skills and providing a platform to stretch their creativity to not only prepare them for success, but to develop them into an exceptional fit for their company.

At Vector, we recruit high school graduates and college students to introduce people to Cutco® Cutlery. We have approximately 250 District offices who recruit in a decentralized manner. Cutco® was established in 1949 and is now the largest manufacturer of kitchen cutlery in the United States and Canada.

When our people thrive, we thrive.

Skills for life

Employers across the globe are expressing frustration in the lack of soft skills found in young professionals today. According to a LinkedIn study of hiring managers, 59 percent said soft skills were difficult to find and this skill gap was limiting their productivity. Others said soft skills are increasingly tougher to find than hard skills, yet their importance is greater (Berger, 2016). That's a problem.

At Vector Marketing, we don't merely recruit people to sell Cutco®; we channel our efforts toward a resolution. Our mission is to recruit students looking to apply their skills and simultaneously unearth qualities previously unrevealed in themselves. We aim to break the stigmas surrounding sales and allow students to see how many soft skills they can hone through something they never thought they'd do: sell knives. We provide a platform that allows students to practice communication with people and implement a range of learned skills. Our representatives often report augmentation in their abilities to listen, set goals, perform presentations, handle rejection, and manage their time, amongst an array of others. Their confidence sky rockets, their social proficiencies amplify, and we become proud parents.

Students will learn the importance of listening to customers, decipher what they say, and then discover how this aptitude applies to everyday life. Working with Vector Marketing will show students how *setting* goals is vital to achieving them. By setting goals, we transform our wishes into achievements. As a result, goals are achieved, and we begin to believe in our abilities to not only sell, but communicate.

Many students admit to a fear of public speaking, but few are taking active steps in overcoming this trepidation. Sales is a great place to take control of this apprehension. By stepping out of their familiar realms, our apprentices will discover the power within themselves and the normality of public communication. Inevitably, the art of sales is coupled with either a polite no-thank-you or an occasional aggressive rebuff. On either side of the coin, representatives become masters in handling opposition. Not only is this an applicable tool in the professional world, but it is an essential life skill. It is human nature to avoid rejection, but it is also human nature to discard what we do not know, understand, or care for. Acquiring the capability to handle refutation improves an individual's confidence and avoids potential setbacks.

Finally, Vector Marketing sales representatives become warriors of time management, perhaps the paramount, versatile expertise achieved. As autonomy increases, time management becomes a vital part of one's job description. By learning to plan, schedule, and manage their own time, students become increasingly efficient and valuable. This skill is not only important in the sales world but in nearly every aspect of life.

The direct sales façade

Scarcely any college students verbalize an aspiration to work in sales. The question is why. I have a few theories, but ultimately all signs point to a main idea: they are unaware that sales can exercise their skills and knowledge acquired in school. Whether a student is undecided on a career path or on track to becoming a doctor, working in sales will be nothing short of supplemental in their efforts to achieve their goals.

Unfortunately, the sales/direct sales market is flooded with misconceptions and surrounded with stigmas. I often hear, "It's impossible to make money," or "You have to sell to friends and family, and no one will give you the time of day," and "It's a pyramid scheme, therefore it's illegal." When people are under these pretenses about direct sales, they are looking through a clouded lens and miss the true benefits that can be obtained.

Vector Marketing works diligently to clarify these misconceptions and authentically pageant a positive representation of a direct sales company. We have a braided focus: quality product, superior customer treatment, and care for our sales representatives. For people—potential customers and representatives alike—to see the true heart of Vector, we actively work with marketing organizations, our representatives on college campuses, and several high school organizations, providing both students and administrators the opportunity to see beyond any preconceived notion regarding direct sales.

How Vector overcomes

Marketing organizations

We work with two main marketing organizations: Pi Sigma Epsilon, the only sales and marketing fraternity in the country, and DECA. Our involvement with both parties gives us a reputable platform to demonstrate the values of Vector, whether it be volunteering and teaching skills for life, skills for competitions, or mentoring students to further develop their proficiencies. As students repeatedly meet with our representatives and see our postings, we become recognizable and memorable developing a rich source for recruits. When we recruit sales representatives, we postulate opportunity for growth as we promote exclusively from within.

Student ambassadors

Since word-of-mouth is our prime form of sales, we have sales representatives who double as student ambassadors on campuses that work with the local manager to assist with recruiting, training, and managing. By adding another channel for students to discover and identify Vector Marketing, we increase our opportunity to find prospective sales candidates.

Sincerely direct

Many misconceptions about direct sales come from a lack of understanding of what "direct sales" really means. To further overcome the misconceptions, our sales representatives sell *directly* to the customer; there is no store front or middle man. This arrangement amplifies quality and personalized interaction between our customers and our sales representatives.

Academia

At Vector, we work with branding at both the student and academia level. For over 30 years, we have had an Academic Advisory Board comprised of professors from around the country to advise on training programs, recruiting on campuses, and more. We are also heavily involved with career centers on campuses throughout high schools, colleges, and our professional organizations. Our involvement allows us to answer questions and become directly involved in recruiting activities, simultaneously allowing us to work shoulder-to-shoulder with the students.

So, how are we winning the talent war? By showing and enhancing students' capabilities, transforming them into not only stronger sales people, but better communicators, listeners, professionals, and individuals of the world. We have a family atmosphere that allows them to channel their skills with rapid opportunity for advancement from sales representative to managerial training, as we promote exclusively from within. I began working for Vector as a student 25 years ago, never imagining myself where I am today, and I wouldn't trade it. Even our company presidents started as sales representatives and continue to apply the skills they learned in their present positions. So, although students may not originally see themselves beyond their first summer with us, the skills they will develop will carry them into their next endeavor with confidence. We believe after working with us, students will see beyond their immediate future and envision what their prospective future could hold with Vector Marketing on their side.

References:

Dishman, Lydia. (2017, January 05). How the Gig Economy Will Change In 2017 | Fast Company | The Future of Business. Retrieved March 08, 2017, from https://www.fastcompany.com/3066905/how-the-gig-economy-will-change-in-2017

Buchanan, Leigh. (2016, November 30). State of Entrepreneurship 2017: Growing Revenue, Growing Uncertainty. Retrieved March 08, 2017, from http://www.inc.com/magazine/201612/leigh-buchanan/state-of-entrepreneurship-2017.html

Berger Ph.D., Guy. (2016, August 30). Soft Skills Are Increasingly Crucial to Getting Your Dream Job. LinkedIn.com

Comparing Apples and Chickens: Why Students' Expectations of the Candidate Experience are SO Different from Those of Experienced Job Seekers?

Mary Scott

As a consultant who advises employers on college student candidate experience best practices – and as someone who began her corporate career as a recruiter – I have long recognized the challenges and frustrations inherent in applying the sourcing tools and strategies appropriate for the experienced job seeker marketplace to the campus environment. What, on its face, appears simply to be a variation on a theme – just engaging with candidates at a different stage of life – is indeed a very different journey, and requires a full understanding of the unique expectations of students during their job search, along with the attitudes and experiences that shape their perspectives and opinions.

Those who will benefit most from reading this chapter are recruiters and hiring managers who are accustomed to the experienced talent acquisition marketplace, and have additional responsibility for their organization's university relations and recruitment hiring. It will also be useful for those in the professional seeking to strengthen their competitiveness with campus talent. The focus of this chapter is candidate touchpoints – how and why they differ for college students, in comparison with experienced job seekers – rather than employers' internal staffing processes. The specific areas to be explored are: candidate attraction; the application process; interviewing considerations; and the offer process.

The source for the findings presented in this essay is a research project – 'Students Benchmark the Candidate Experience' – conducted by Scott Resource Group on behalf of a consortium of sponsoring employers[1] during the first quarter of 2015. An important caveat to bear in mind: The students who participated in the research project attended universities[2] that are targeted by leading employers as key sources of campus talent, and the findings throughout this essay will reflect their experience base. Whereas the attitudes and expectations discussed herein may well be relevant for the broader university population, the findings have not been validated outside the parameters of the original study.

Candidate attraction

A key differentiator between hiring experienced candidates, and their campus counterparts, maps to a simple but fundamental distinction: Whereas those who have established a workplace track record more typically are focusing on a narrow spectrum of next steps (be it a specific job and/or targeting a few desirable companies), college students are more likely to be 'playing the field', and exploring opportunities at a range of potential employers – as well as a variety of jobs. This has a significant impact on the candidate attraction continuum, including [but certainly not limited to] these elements:

- According to students, their **university job board** is a go-to one-stop-shop that not only lists entry-level jobs – but indicates an interest on behalf of the employer in considering applicants from their school. This stands in stark contrast to commercial job boards that tend to frustrate students because they target experienced candidates; even those positions marked 'entry-level' often require at least a year of relevant work history.

- Incumbent on the employer in **posting a job** on a career services site is assuring that the wording itself can be understood by students who a] may be wholly unfamiliar with the position descriptors and qualifications; and b] most likely are clueless about an organization's jargon, including acronyms. I was reminded of this during a focus group discussion recently, when a business student commented on a position description she had read that that stated "You'll be analyzing…" and several others nodded in agreement when she exclaimed: "What does that even MEAN?" Experienced candidates have a frame of reference that informs their understanding of employers' job descriptions, but students – even those who have interned – often lack that context. When in doubt, ask a recent college hire to review your job posting, and edit accordingly.

- **Word-of-mouth** is a powerful employer brand influencer on campus. Students freely share their own experiences with specific employers' recruitment practices [for better and for worse] as well as their take on the desirability of working for a company, based on the impact of their internship[s]. While such promoter/detractor commentary certainly occurs in the experienced hire marketplace, it is typically part of an informal chat among acquaintances. On campus, however, there is a critical mass of job seekers who are particularly vocal about their experiences with, and impressions of, specific employers based on their candidate journey. And the resulting perceptions about a company's desirability as a potential employer can be enormously impacted by such student reviews – because they are viewed among their classmates as highly credible sources of information.

- Many employers seeking undergraduate college talent assume that they only need attend the campus **career fair** to attract targeted students. Keep in mind that these students are shopping for opportunities at many other organizations as well, and that a firm's appeal is based primarily on the interaction attendees have with its representatives – not the design of its booth or 'coolness' of its giveaway. A widespread complaint among students who have attended campus career fairs is the commonplace rejoinder they hear from representatives to "go the website" to find answers to any and all questions, and to fill out an online application. This leads them to question why the company bothered to attend the event. It is such a toxic practice that I consider it a top-ranked employer brand killer. Experienced candidates typically do not rely on job fairs to identify potential employers consistent with their younger counterparts – and success in attracting students at such an event requires a thorough understanding of the behaviors and practices that telegraph interest in the attendees – and those that suggest quite the opposite.

The Application Process

Experienced and student candidates alike rely on employers' websites for a wide range of information – and use the portal to apply for opportunities.

And herein lies a significant difference in students' needs and expectations, in comparison with their experienced counterparts:

- Chief among students' issues with the online application process [which could be a book chapter in and of itself] is simply this: With the exception of those employers that have invested in tailoring their website to the college market, the job opportunity exploration and application process can be enormously frustrating. A lack of appropriate **filtering options** is a major source of dissatisfaction among students at all levels. They need and expect to be able to sort through opportunities based on such important differentiators as degree level, full-time and intern positions, and geographical location – and most basic of all: Whether the positions are for full-time candidates or for students. A generic jobs page is simply not useful to students, nor is the limiting factor of only applying for one job at a time. It is unlikely that an experienced candidate would encounter such challenges in navigating an employer's website, which underscores the appropriateness of the design to that cohort – with the assumption that students' needs and expectations are the same. Nothing could be further from the truth.

- Another application process expectation that differentiates students from experienced candidates relates to the length and depth of the **online form** itself. Whereas the latter may also be annoyed with detailed queries about such required fields as last five addresses and contact information for prior managers, students see such questions as a reflection that the company doesn't understand their stage of (work) life. Given that most of them have applied to college recently using the Common Application[3] they are mystified as to why they are being put through such administrative hoops, with a significant percentage (ranging from 55% for surveyed Liberal Arts majors to 70% of IT/CS students) indicating that they have given up on completing an online application.

- Students also value '**Day in the Life**' videos on employer websites, to help them understand the reality of the workplace. Such videos must be authentic and credible; students can easily detect overproduced corporate marketing clips, which are often viewed as dishonest, thereby damaging the company brand. Experienced candidates have their own workplace knowledge base to inform their expectations; students – even those who have interned – do not have that baseline awareness.

Interviewing

A fundamental difference inherent in the college student recruitment model at most schools – that does not have an experienced hiring corollary – is the practice of screening candidates during an on-campus interview. It is important to recognize the expectations students have if they are indeed engaged in a one-on-one campus discussion.

- The timing of the campus interview "high season" has shifted dramatically over the past several years. Whereas it was commonplace for graduating students to be available for, and interested in, spring semester interviews in the not-so-distant past, there has been a wholesale reworking of the timeline, such that interviews – even for internship opportunities on many campuses – now take place in the fall, and during a highly-compressed window, at that. This is not only a surprise for many employers – but a daunting challenge when actual start dates are many months off. It is imperative, however, to close the loop with students who are interviewed on campus early in the school year; the occurrence of candidates not receiving a decision until closer to the end of second semester [if at all] happens all too frequently – and is a significant dissatisfier that rarely results in an acceptance on the part of the candidate who has long ago assumed a lack of interest.

- Students infer a palpable interest [or lack of same] in them as individuals based not only on the above timing and response considerations, but on the venue or tool used to conduct the interview. On those campuses where interviews are commonplace, there is an expectation that employers who are truly interested in hiring their students will invest the face time: personal contact is a compelling differentiator, as students compare their experiences with competing firms. If the employer chooses to conduct phone or

Internet interviews in lieu of visiting campus, it is critical that all logistical and technical details be executed professionally. And employers send a signal about their seriousness in recruiting students based on the medium they choose. One focus group participant commented on how turned off he was to a company that offered only a phone interview – because said employer was located across the street from campus. He declined the opportunity to interview with them, because he assumed a lukewarm interest in his application, at best.

Offer process

Another essential difference in the experienced versus student hiring process – and one associated with the discussion of interviewing practices above – maps to candidate disposition. The issue here is not the communication of a lack of fit [all candidates value receiving such news, and the sooner the better], but rather the expectation of a suitable timeframe to consider the offer – and the extended period between acceptance and start date, to wit:

- A unique [and usually once-in-a-lifetime] opportunity afforded to students is having a chance to consider a wide range of jobs and potential employers before making the decision as to their post-graduation direction – and the topic of many a focus group discussion has been the desire to "get it right". Whereas many students certainly understand the business need of employers to secure the commitment of those to whom they extend offers, there is a growing resentment stemming from the practice of only allowing an **abbreviated timeframe** to make such an important choice, which is commonplace among experienced candidates. Students, on the other hand, express a desire to explore their options, and are particularly annoyed when their offer expires the day before their campus career fair. They see such a practice as opaque and manipulative, and consider reneging on their commitment, should it come to that, as fair retribution. Many universities have policies in place to manage the offer acceptance timeframe, and employers should have full knowledge of [and abide by] these guidelines. The damage done by employers who attempt to "lock down" targeted candidates has been a vigorous discussion point on many campuses lately, and understandably so.

- Yet another distinguishing characteristic of the campus candidate population flows from the offer extension timeframe – It's commonplace for students to accept an offer of employment many months before their actual start date, a condition that rarely occurs in the experienced hiring marketplace. For this reason, it is highly recommended that employers have a strategy to **"keep warm"** those who are planning to join them following graduation This can take many forms – "care packages" at exam time, including the new hires in campus recruiting events, inviting them to take part in company functions, keeping them updated about company news - but the underlying precept is that students "feel the love", and are as excited on their first day of work as they were the day they accepted their offer.

Final thoughts

The premise of this essay is straightforward – That although there are certainly basic similarities [e.g. filling a position] in hiring experienced candidates, as compared with their yet-to-graduate counterparts, there are a number of fundamental differences that need to be considered and acted on when targeting campus talent. Listening to students in hundreds of focus groups all over the country has convinced me that it's both understandable that many employers don't grasp the nuances – and obvious why students are frustrated by those that lack such a perspective.

What's apparent to me, as a recruiter in a previous life, is the basic difference that drives experienced and campus hiring: The former is primarily tactical, while the latter is – or should be – strategic at its core. The observations detailed in this chapter are not intended to be all-encompassing, but they do reflect the practices of employers that enjoy success in recruiting campus talent. And I state, this is based on what I hear directly from students, not as a prescription based in theory or conventional wisdom.

Filling a talent pipeline with bright and enthusiastic college graduates is a challenge, and one that is at once richly rewarding – and much more difficult to execute than many assume. Understanding and acting on the unique needs and expectations of this cohort will provide an important framework on which to build a competitive and enduring campus program – regardless of size or scope – and position employers to attract and hire graduating students to meet their entry-level talent needs.

Endnotes:

[1] ADP, Cummins, Deloitte, Enterprise, EY, Fidelity Investments, KPMG, Macy's, MIT Lincoln Labs

[2] Boston College, Cal – Berkeley, Cal State – Fullerton, Cornell, Duke [Fuqua], Georgia Tech, Illinois – Urbana/Champaign, Indiana [Kelley], Michigan – Ann Arbor [Ross], MIT, Notre Dame [Mendoza], NYU, Ohio State, Penn State, Purdue, Stanford, Syracuse, Texas – Austin, Texas A&M, Virginia Tech, Wisconsin – Madison

[3] An online undergraduate college application accepted by over 400 independent colleges.

Offer Policies: Time for Different Thinking?

Aaron Goldberg

A great relationship between a university and an employer is a beautiful thing. The two move together; they communicate and focus on opportunities to realize shared goals. That relationship is one of the reasons why we enjoy this work. We come from separate worlds but need each other and our respective expertise. Like any relationship, we have moments where disagreements occur. We've all either made or received that call, a violation of the university's offer policy has occurred. Is it time revisit that conversation? Do offer policies work?

Consideration #1: What are we teaching?

If the writer or reader of this piece were to receive an offer of employment tomorrow, the terms of that offer would be dictated by industry norms and market conditions. If career readiness is the goal of a university's career center, then we must ask ourselves if the hiring policies that guide our work are aligned to that goal. All aspects of our modern lives involve making difficult decisions with limited time and information. Would we not prefer to have students make difficult decisions in real time with the support of dedicated and capable career center partners? Can we find opportunities to build that skillset into our definition of career readiness?

Employers are expressly seeking entry level talent that can operate and excel in environments with limited information. The process of conducting due diligence, reviewing facts and opinions and making a decision are immediately useful in any industry or work environment. Our goal should be to use the full-time employment process to model those skills and not allow students to lean on school policies to delay a difficult decision.

The conversation around millennial talent in corporate America tends to disparage student's lack of grit or perseverance. While not their intention, university hiring policies often reinforce that stereotype. If we don't want our students to require handholding, then we shouldn't be holding their hands.

Consideration #2: Campus recruiting is changing (and quickly)

When those unfamiliar with the norms of campus recruiting confront these policies, often the initial reaction is shock. After a lengthy recruiting process, filled with presentations, job shadows, coffee chats, mock interviews, social outings and more, hiring managers are frustrated by offer deadlines that allow competitors ample time to identify students that a company has invested in and leverage that investment. This frustration is particularly impactful as it affects companies who do the right thing. They exhibit all the right behaviors, they follow policies, and they invest in creating mutually beneficial career experiences for students. They develop these students and impart technical and soft skills, but make those students more marketable in the process.

This dynamic is amplified by the changes in campus recruiting. Timelines have shifted in many industries. Digitization has further destabilized timelines, allowing for students to apply and be interviewed year-round. Some firms have made the decision to opt out of on-campus interviews. School policies have tried to account for this by moving to a "catch all" model. Whereas policies used to apply to on-campus recruiting only, universities now cover all students under offer policies regardless of the location of the interview. This incremental approach to policy change is a temporary solution.

Employers are also busy creating more bespoke programming, allowing students the opportunity to try different businesses or functions or geographies. Multi-year internship programs that now proliferate among more sophisticated employers are not accounted for in current offer policies. If a firm develops a rising junior through a sophomore internship program, should the return offer for the rising senior internship be under the same terms as an offer to a student who has no relationship with that employer?

Many practitioners in recruiting make the argument that if a student spends 10 weeks with an employer, learning marketable skills and becoming fluent in that company's culture, then that student should have the information required to either accept an offer quickly or decline that offer and return to the campus recruiting process. After months of recruiting and a full summer internship, what is left to be learned during the months which that offer remains open? How do we account for the students who have less opportunity because their peers are holding multiple offers for the duration of the recruiting season?

The changing landscape of campus recruiting requires that our policies recognize the increasingly nuanced nature of the field. A one size fits all policy is too broad and doesn't acknowledge current practices and market conditions.

Consideration #3: How can we enforce policies?

Enforcing offer policies is hard. I don't envy the university professionals who have to discipline employer partners by limiting that employer's access to students. If the only way to enforce a policy requires that an institution decreases student opportunity that policy is unlikely to be enforced. While the author isn't aware of any data on the subject, anecdotal evidence would suggest that this happens quite rarely. More likely, offer policies are used to create compromise and to give career professionals a framework for negotiating disagreements between academic institutions and corporate partners. Policies have evolved into principles, leaving our industry without the tools to deal with a rapidly changing environment.

Moving forward

When universities confront corporate partners regarding policy violations (or perceived violations), career center professionals often cite two factors as the real reasons why companies should alter their behavior. The first is related to how students perceive an employer's brand and values. The second is the threat of a high renege rate, creating a situation where the best candidates have accepted offers and employers are left with open positions in their programs.

The future of university and employer policies needs to focus on these concerns as they represent real downsides for employers and universities. Students need to learn that a company's values should influence all aspects of its operations, including the campus recruiting process. If a company, in its pitch to students, claims to espouse certain values and those values are not realized in the recruiting process, students should understand that perhaps that employer is not a best fit for that student. While that may create a situation where students need to make difficult decisions, we should support and embrace that process as it is part of normal employer and potential employee discourse. The point of the process is that students need to vet employers thoughtfully. A company's actions should match their words and relying on policies to prevent a company's real culture from coming through might be a disservice to students who need to learn how to read such signals. By removing narrow policies and allowing students to see how a company operates in real time, students can make better decisions about best fit.

The threat of student's renege should also temper a company's desire to explode offers or otherwise violate the guiding principles that we all agree on. We should consider allowing this to happen and allowing the market to identify companies who do not abide by the norms and expectations of students.

Protections do need to exist and universities should have the right to welcome and not welcome any employer on-campus. But by shielding students from bad companies, well-meaning career center professionals are masking company's true behaviors from students who need to be able to judge those behaviors as part of the recruiting process.

At the least, as practitioners in this space, we need to acknowledge that current policies do not fit the current environment. Let's come together to realign our policies and guiding principles. Let's develop a framework that positions students to make the best decisions possible but also teaches them the practical skills they need to be successful long term. Let's allow companies to live their values and let students decide who is best in industry and whose values should warrant best talent.

Take Control of Your Employer Brand Using Data

Dustin Clinard and Katharine Lynn

What is Data-Led Employer Branding?

Imagine a world that is getting smarter each day, with companies specializing in the skills required to beat competition and talent having access to more tools to advance their careers. Imagine, also, that both companies and talent have data to make decisions about who is likely to succeed in a role and what role fits best for a particular person. So far, these imagined scenarios probably haven't impressed you – they might even seem logical. Now think of one of the few areas that exist for companies to stand out to both current and future talent and it's not difficult to understand what this chapter is about – the growing importance of data in employer branding.

Employer branding has been growing in importance, and quickly. More than 300,000 people list "employer branding" as a skill or title on LinkedIn. The function is becoming more prevalent and more clearly defined as a separate role within organizations. There is also more management-level attention on the topic, with C-level executives becoming increasingly concerned about the availability of key skills. But what is employer branding, aside from the standard "it's what talent thinks about you as an employer" answer? Well, as with many things in life – it depends. To some, employer branding takes the form of great internal talent engagement programs. To others, it's a slick recruitment marketing campaign to attract talent, or possibly a great campus recruiting strategy combined with great social media execution. These are all pieces of the puzzle; however, the undisputable conclusion is that data is playing an increasing role in separating the best from the rest.

For organizations, the benefits of investing in employer branding are clear: in simple terms, a strong employer brand leads to happier and more productive employees, lower turnover, reduced costs, and higher profits. More specifically, according to a 2011 LinkedIn survey, companies with a strong employer brand benefited from a cost of hire that was two times lower than those with weaker employer brands. On top of that, companies with strong employer brands enjoy a much lower employee turnover rate (28%), which results in a significant cost savings.

A strong employer brand is also beneficial from a talent perspective. Universum's annual research shows that the average number of employers students would consider working for has consistently increased in recent years – 23.7 in 2016, up from 18.4 in 2012. For high-demand majors like computer science students, these numbers are even higher. While there are many factors at play, this could indicate confusion on students' part about what opportunities are available to them, or what different employers stand for. A strong employer brand is proven to help students self-select into – or, just as importantly, out of – opportunities that may or may not be right for them.

"Without data, you're just another person with an opinion." (W. Edwards Deming)

Gathering data for use in employer branding work: why it matters, and how it's unique

"Big Data" has been a buzzword of choice for many years, and with good reason. Companies simply no longer make decisions without relying on data, especially as technology advances and offers more, better, and faster data. However, there are some pretty divergent opinions on what makes big data truly "big" (which we're not attempting to solve here), and add to that the importance of a career or employment choice and you might see why data can be tough to collect and trust in the employer branding field. That said, amidst the growing trend, great progress has been made in the HR space (for example, HR Analytics is now an expected corporate position).

Unfortunately, too many companies attempt to build and manage their employer brands without using data, relying instead on opinions and feelings from those who believe they know the culture. Employer branding can be a nebulous and subjective space, in part because it lacks clear ownership and outputs. Many companies know at an instinctual level that they need an employer brand, but lack the clear definition, goals, and measurements around employer brand that exist for other company functions. Seasoned marketers, for example, would never launch a product or run an advertising campaign without investing heavily in understanding the market; in other words, in using data to uncover what its target customers want. Instead, they would conduct loads of market research, build target buyer personas, and develop marketing campaigns based on the uncovered insights. Employer branding must be, but often isn't, approached with the same level of scrutiny.

How is employer branding data collected?

A layered approach to brand

For organizations that appreciate the need to base their employer branding decisions on data, the obvious follow up questions becomes: *How?*

The core of a data-driven employer brand is the EVP (*employer value proposition*). Universum defines the EVP as the unique set of offerings, associations, and values that an organization should use to positively influence the right potential candidates and current employees. It provides a long-term foundation and strategic framework for employer branding efforts. It's also important to note that a company's EVP is *not* its employer brand. The EVP is not a tagline, a campaign, or a visual expression. Rather, the EVP provides the underlying content that is then transformed into messages, ads, and a communication strategy for the employer brand. You may of course have a tagline and express your brand visually, however the subtle distinctions are important as they not only lead to better results but also more buy-in from critical stakeholders.

The EVP Development

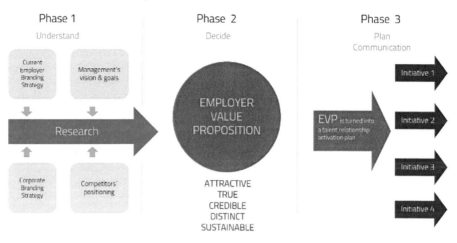

This graphic describes the process Universum uses to develop a company's EVP, using both internal and external data and validating it along the way.

Universum's process incorporates five critical factors into an EVP: what's *true* about the employee experience, what's *attractive* to potential candidates, what's *credible* and associated with the organization, what's *sustainable* with the long-term aspiration of the organization, and what's *distinct* about the organization. Each of these components serves a unique purpose and is critical to establishing a strong employer branding foundation.

Methods of data collection

There are many ways to collect this data. In order to track the *external perspective*, organizations like Universum rely on market research. Universum surveys upwards of 1.5 million students and professionals annually to understand their career goals and motivations, as well as their perceptions about specific employers. This kind of data can reveal interesting insights about the state of the talent market. For example, according to Universum's most recent research, a global shift has started towards a desire for organizations with an inspiring purpose, with less importance placed on a company's products or services.

It's important to note that, while these trends are important to track, the data must be consumed within the right individual context. There are countless studies that have been published about the Millennial generation, or Generation Z that followed. It would be a mistake to try to use these large-scale studies to make decisions at a company level. Universum's research *also* reveals striking differences in talent preferences among different target groups. For example, while it might appear that potential candidates care most about leadership opportunities, when we look at more specific drill downs – students of a particular major, or students attending a particular university – the data can look quite different.

Interestingly, while the internal data is more readily available to companies, it is often more challenging to collect. Organizations often collect employee data on their own, at least in a very basic way – an annual engagement survey, for example – but it's really difficult to elicit honest responses from current employees. Out of concern for job security or negative backlash, employees sometimes distrust internal surveys – even those that claim to be anonymous. Using an independent third-party to collect internal employee data can be much more beneficial in terms of collecting honest responses.

This data collection can take many forms, depending on what questions an employer is hoping to answer. Engagement surveys are extremely useful as a "pulse check" each year, to ensure overall satisfaction of employees. For a deeper dive into the employee experiences, internal surveys or focus groups can provide really interesting insights. These can provide deeper, qualitative feedback on issues that arise in the engagement survey; they can also provide pointed answers to questions about specific programs or offerings. Companies can, for example, run a focus group with interns about their experiences in an internship program, or survey candidates who declined offers to gain a more robust understanding of what went wrong.

It's not simply a one-time effort.

One of the more common mistakes organizations make when it comes to their employer brand is to treat it as a one-off project. When done properly, employer branding is not a project that has a beginning and an end - it is a long-term, strategic, iterative process. The employer brand should be visible in every part of the company, and for that reason, the data collection process needs to be constant. Data should not just be used to *build* the brand; it should be used to constantly validate, measure, and tweak the brand.

Data vs. intuition: Examples of why employer branding data matters

To conclude, we'll leave you with a few examples of how a strong, data-backed brand can lead to better outcomes for organizations of all shapes and sizes.

Scenario 1: Your messaging isn't hitting the target.

Take the example of a large, global conglomerate in the manufacturing industry - we'll call it Company A. Like many organizations, Company A is in desperate need of technical skills, and has therefore been on a journey to change its brand perceptions from a traditional industrial giant to a tech company. In order to do this, Company A started by measuring its current brand perceptions – what potential candidates believe to be true about the company today.

Top 10 most associated attributes with Company XYZ

1. Market success
2. Good reference for future career
3. Clear path for advancement
4. Innovation
4. Interaction with international clients and colleagues
4. Leaders who will support my development
7. Team-oriented work
8. Recognizing performance (meritocracy)
9. Prestige
10. A creative and dynamic work environment

This figure presents the top 10 attributes the target group associates with Company A.

Not surprisingly, the perceptions were what you might expect for a large, stable manufacturing giant. Company A knew immediately that, while some of these perceptions were true, some needed to be corrected – especially in order to attract the tech talent it was after. Company A looked first at what computer science students were most interested in:

Top preferences | Engineering/IT

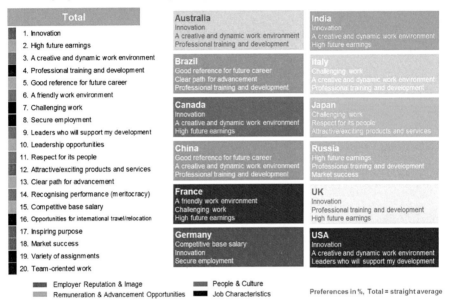

Total	Australia	India
1. Innovation	Innovation	Innovation
2. High future earnings	A creative and dynamic work environment	A creative and dynamic work environment
3. A creative and dynamic work environment	Professional training and development	High future earnings
4. Professional training and development	**Brazil**	**Italy**
5. Good reference for future career	Good reference for future career	Challenging work
6. A friendly work environment	Clear path for advancement	A creative and dynamic work environment
7. Challenging work	Professional training and development	Professional training and development
8. Secure employment	**Canada**	**Japan**
9. Leaders who will support my development	Innovation	Challenging work
10. Leadership opportunities	A creative and dynamic work environment	Respect for its people
11. Respect for its people	High future earnings	Attractive/exciting products and services
12. Attractive/exciting products and services	**China**	**Russia**
13. Clear path for advancement	Good reference for future career	High future earnings
14. Recognising performance (meritocracy)	A creative and dynamic work environment	Professional training and development
15. Competitive base salary	Professional training and development	Market success
16. Opportunities for international travel/relocation	**France**	**UK**
17. Inspiring purpose	A friendly work environment	Innovation
18. Market success	Challenging work	Professional training and development
19. Variety of assignments	High future earnings	High future earnings
20. Team-oriented work	**Germany**	**USA**
	Competitive base salary	Innovation
	Innovation	A creative and dynamic work environment
	Secure employment	Leaders who will support my development

Employer Reputation & Image   People & Culture
Remuneration & Advancement Opportunities   Job Characteristics   Preferences in %, Total = straight average

This figure presents the top 10 attributes preferred by STEM talent in various countries.

Again, not surprising – it's pretty commonly known that tech talent values attributes like innovation, creativity, and autonomy. As a final step, Company A looked at what its target talent – computer science students at its specific target schools – desire most in an employer.

In doing so, it became clear that the preferences of this drilled-down target group look a lot different from the general population. Had Company A not looked first properly defined a target group, and made an effort to truly understand its target market, it would have launched a branding campaign that was totally off the mark. Instead, Company A was able to use the data to create a more informed branding campaign that appealed deeply to its target group.

Scenario 2: Your global brand health is out of whack.

Universum recently worked with another large, global company in the retail space. The organization (we'll call it Company B) recently decided it was going to change recruiting models – beginning a shift away from hiring only college students to taking a more holistic approach around the world. In order to make this transition successfully, Company B needed a rock-solid understanding of what kinds of candidates would be successful in the organization in all of its operating markets. In order to do this, the company embarked on a thorough and expansive research project: identifying its top performers internally and gaining an understanding of their motivations, investigating the external perceptions of the organization, comparing the results around the world to find the difference between global scale and local nuance, and creating a tool to help its recruiters better identify the right talent in each market.

It was a huge undertaking, but has truly expedited and improved its recruitment process. Plus, Company B plans to validate this data annually. By taking snapshots every year – not only of its current brand perceptions, but also of the drivers of its most successful employees – Company B will be able to benchmark its incremental progress. The year-on-year changes, while subtle, will be distinct – and the effort required to manage the incremental change will be much less significant than waiting several years without tracking. Measuring progress will provide important perspective and, ultimately, require less effort to maintain.

Scenario 3: Your recruitment decisions are contentious and not achieving results.

For a final example, take Company C – a Midwestern automotive company with a serious need for smart, young engineering talent. While Company C has a strong brand name, it is no longer perceived as an innovative or future-focused company – and therefore, was struggling to attract the talent it needs. Plus, its recruitment efforts were not very strong – the company was spread out at many schools across the country, equipped with weak recruitment marketing materials, and was approaching its recruitment efforts with a lot of inconsistency.

Universum's approach was twofold. First, Company C needed to focus its efforts to fewer schools that would yield higher quality, better fit candidates. The company used data (e.g. rankings, size and make-up of the enrollment and graduating classes, currently employed alumni performance) to make this decision – removing the sometimes, emotional component of school selection – resulting in a more strategic presence at fewer schools.

Next, Company C needed to sharpen its messaging and better align it to what its target talent was interested in. This resulted in more appealing messages that were more consistent across its schools. Both of these efforts resulted in an overall stronger employer brand.

Use data to drive the brand forward

Employer branding is part art – there are still many ways subjectivity enters the decision-making process about where, when, and how to present your company as an employer. However, the increasing availability and belief in data is changing the landscape to enable companies to build strong and sustainable data-led employer brands. As a leading expert in the field, Universum has seen first-hand how that leads to happier and more productive employees, lower turnover, reduced costs, and higher profits.

Successful College Recruiting for the Brand-Challenged

Glen Fowler

Brand name organizations are generally inundated with talented candidates' resumes and applications. Talented candidates search online for these organizations' open positions, and they anxiously line up at the career events to meet with the organizations' recruiters. In contrast, organizations with little brand recognition do not have the luxury of having names that, in and of themselves, attract an ample candidate pool from which to hire. Instead, to successfully compete for talented candidates, recruiters at such organizations need to execute more creative relationship-driven recruiting strategies. Specifically, the organizations' recruiting success hinges on the recruiters' networking, the recruiters' and the organizations' credibility, and the experience the organizations provide to candidates.

Assessing the degree to which an organization is brand-challenged is the first step

For simplicity sake, I'll refer to brand-challenged organizations as **BCOs**. When recruiters first accept positions with organizations, they cannot assume that those organizations are NOT BCOs based simply on their own experiences. In fact, new recruiters often hold positive biases about their organizations for a number of reasons, including the fact that they believe enough in the organizations to have aligned themselves with them. Further, recruiters may believe that organizations are familiar brands because of their own level of awareness of those organizations. However, that awareness might be caused by their organizations' statuses within particular industries or regions.

Thus, rather than relying on their own instincts to identify if organizations are BCOs, recruiters must assess the brand through potential candidates' eyes and understand and appreciate the candidates' perspectives—regardless of whether those perspectives are warranted. It doesn't matter if an organization's brand is commonly known among the elderly or in certain regions; the key is whether or not the organization's brand is familiar to its targeted candidates' demographic.

For example, my organization—the California State Auditor's Office—has a brand that is very well known within our industry: we're considered a leader in auditing circles. Nonetheless, most candidates know little about our industry and therefore have not heard about our organization. Further, many candidates misunderstand our organizational brand: they assume that we must audit individual or corporate tax issues and that we exclusively hire accounting majors. I initially had the same impression when I first learned about the organization many years ago. The recruiter at that time quickly dispelled my preconceived notions of auditing. She "taught" me that the organization conducts both financial and performance audits of government agencies, as well as investigations of governmental wrongdoing—and that it does not conduct tax audits.

Also, recruiters need to recognize that organizations might be brand-challenged not due to a lack of recognition, but because of legal challenges, customer complaints, scandals, or other compromised business/ethical practices. I strongly suspect that recruiting managers with mega-brand organizations like Volkswagen and Wells Fargo pivoted and revised their recruiting strategies after dealing with their organizations' legal issues. In such cases, recruiters need to not only follow the BCO strategies outlined below, but also need to fully understand their organizations' positions about the issues so they can appropriately and adequately address candidates' questions and concerns.

Networking is the critical to a BCO's recruiting strategy

Merriam-Webster's defines *networking* in part as "the cultivation of productive relationships for employment or business." Experienced BCO recruiters recognize that they cannot effectively recruit talented college students on their own and that "productive relationships"—which I'll refer to as *partnerships*—are critical to successful recruiting campaigns. Successful BCO recruiters must foster partnerships with many college representatives, including career center directors, counselors, employer relations representatives, and faculty, among others. The goal of such partnerships is pairing students with positions for which they are both qualified and an appropriate fit.

Further, many of these partnerships may evolve into personal relationships as well over time. Toward this end, I meet with many college representatives for coffee before or after recruiting events when I'm on campus. Our discussions revolve mostly around work topics, like the reports my organization has recently issued, industry challenges and opportunities, and the best ways we can work with each other to find positions for their students. However, we also share updates about our personal lives, families, and yes, pets. The conversations I have with these college representatives are not superficial. We're genuinely interested in and care about each other. These relationships are the primary reason why I have made a career in recruiting and continue to be passionate about it today.

It's equally important that BCO recruiters establish relationships with the advisors and leaders of college groups and associations. In these relationships, the BCO recruiters should serve as resources. They should assist the associations' members in developing life skills, regardless of whether the members are interested in pursuing positions with the recruiters' organizations. Having a sustained presence with these associations is critical. Association advisors and leaders frown upon recruiters who request to present to or participate in functions only when their organizations have vacant positions to fill.

Consistency is key in building relationships

When it comes to partnerships, the most valued relationships are those in which a genuine commitment exists. For BCOs, this means establishing a consistent presence at colleges. What's especially important for BCOs is that their sustained presence needs to involve more than just the organizations themselves; it should involve their recruiters. Strong partnerships can only be achieved and maintained by having BCOs' recruiters serve for an extended period of time, preferably through many recruiting cycles.

Until about fifteen years ago, my organization's practice was to rotate the recruiter position each year. After having been an auditor and then a member of our executive management team, I was asked to serve in this recruiter position. However, after a year, I requested to continue in the role because I had made so many meaningful relationships with representatives at numerous schools—and I couldn't imagine not continuing those relationships. The

State Auditor agreed, recognizing the value of the partnerships I'd established. Having supportive executive management is imperative to the success of any BCO recruiting program. It includes routinely deliberating and strategizing, and committing the necessary resources for the BCO to best recruit talented college candidates.

When BCOs rotate the recruiter role among their employees, it fractures the relationships between the BCOs and the college representatives. Rebuilding these relationships after a BCO rotates in a new recruiter requires a lot of time and energy. The new BCO recruiter is now competing against recruiters from organizations with greater brand recognition for college representatives' time and attention.

When replacing a BCO recruiter is unavoidable, the experienced recruiter should personally introduce the new recruiter to the college representatives if possible. This introduction is an endorsement of the new recruiter and is particularly important because truly effective partnerships between college representatives and BCO recruiters hinge on mutual respect and trust.

College representative partners make the best advocates for a BCO

Well-established college representative partners make the best BCO advocates. When conducting presentations and workshops in college classes taught by faculty with whom I have long-standing relationships, I'm especially grateful for the faculties' engagement and for the recruiting that they'll do on our organization's behalf. Oftentimes they'll introduce me by explaining how impressed they are with my organization's work and encouraging students to apply for positions. Occasionally, some express that they'd wished they had known about our organization as a career option when they were students! This endorsement—and partnership—is invaluable.

Further, at many colleges, faculty routinely invite me to take over entire class periods. When given these opportunities, I use a brief portion of the class session to explain how the students can apply for positions with our organization, and I then spend the rest of the time conducting case study workshops with scenarios that engage and challenge the students. The purpose is to enable the students to experience firsthand how staff in my organization problem solve. The students can then use these skills in their college courses and any profession, regardless of whether they're interested in pursuing positions with our organization.

On occasion, college representative partners request that BCO recruiters participate in activities such as mock interviews and resume critiques. These activities are typically time-consuming, and most recruiters consider them low return-on-investment. Nonetheless, assisting college representatives with such activities is incumbent on BCO recruiters as part of a true partnership. It's a small price to pay for having college representatives market the BCO's brand. A few years ago, a college representative said it best when he expressed his appreciation that my recruiting team members were not "sea gull recruiters." When we asked for clarification, he explained that "…some recruiters quickly stop by, drop off their "stuff" [he used another word], and then go on their way".

Experienced BCO recruiters regard their college representative partners as allies in the quest to hire candidates. As such, BCO recruiters ask college representatives about how they, and the candidates, perceive their organizations' brand. Similarly, they ask for candid advice on overcoming any brand misconceptions and improving the brand recognition. Further, successful BCO recruiters consult college representatives, especially career center partners, about best practices for recruiting talented candidates on their campuses. For overall best practices in recruiting, BCO recruiters should reference the National Association of Colleges and Employers (NACE) Standards.

Effective BCO recruiters are credible educators

In her college student surveys, Mary Scott of the Scott Resource Group consistently finds that "students prefer making face-to-face connections" with recruiters. Making these sorts of connections are fairly easy for organizations with high brand recognition: on numerous occasions I've witnessed candidates wait as long as 30 minutes to get one-on-one time with recruiters representing Silicon Valley organizations at career events. In contrast, the BCO recruiters need to stand in front of their display tables and engage prospective candidates who would otherwise pass by.

Thus, often the best opportunity for BCO recruiters to get face-to-face time with candidates is by conducting information sessions and student group workshops—ideal in-person forums where BCO recruiters can educate candidates about their organizations and brands. This "educating" is the most effective form of BCO recruiting. It's the BCO recruiter's job to clearly convey to candidates and college representatives the organization's mission, work product, impact, and culture. The recruiter must also educate the candidates and college representatives about the entry-level positions that the BCO is seeking to fill.

What's most effective is when the BCO recruiter educates college representatives—especially career center directors—who in turn educate counselors, who in turn educate candidates. To increase the likelihood that information will be accurately conveyed throughout this process, BCO recruiters should furnish the college representatives with recruiting brochures that describe their organizations and positions. In fact, BCO recruiters should ideally host tours of their organizations for the college representatives, creating opportunities for the representatives to see the BCOs' offices, meet with their employees, and better understand their cultures. The college representatives can then speak to other representatives and candidates about their experiences, which should be consistent with the organizational information the recruiters share when educating them about the organizations.

The need for consistency in communicating BCOs' brands underscores why it is so important for BCO recruiters to deeply understand and accurately describe their organizations. By doing so, BCO recruiters instill confidence with the college representatives—and they maintain credibility when the candidates the BCOs hire report back to the college representatives about their experiences. If there are inconsistencies, a recruiter's credibility will erode in the eyes of a college representative, who may then be hesitant to market the organization and its vacancies to future candidates.

The best example of a job posting that was explicit about the expectations for a position was Ernest Shackleton's *London Times* newspaper job advertisement for a 1914 ship crew for an expedition to the South Pole. This advertisement supposedly read, "MEN WANTED FOR HAZARDOUS JOURNEY. SMALL WAGES, BITTER COLD, LONG MONTHS OF COMPLETE DARKNESS, CONSTANT DANGER. SAFE RETURN DOUBTFUL.

HONOUR AND RECOGNITION IN CASE OF SUCCESS." (Huntford, 1985, p.386). Further, Shackleton's interviewing and selection methods focused on character and temperament as well as technical ability. This was fortunate, given that one of his ships became trapped in sea ice, and the crew was forced to make their way on foot, and then lifeboats. What's incredible is that although serious injuries and death were common during Antarctic expeditions at this time, Shackleton's entire crew survived. One might attribute this to Shackleton's candid description of what was expected of the crew—he attracted applicants who knew what would truly be expected of them.

In our organization, we recognize that because candidates learn about our job opportunities from numerous marketing channels, they may not be fully educated about the position requirements and challenges. To address this, we include a step in the hiring process when our deputies meet with our candidates and discuss expectations beyond the required knowledge, skills, and abilities. We want to make sure our candidates fully appreciate both the opportunities our positions offer—like career advancement—and their challenges—like travel and overtime. Just like Ernest Shackleton, we want to make sure our new hires truly know what will be expected of them. Closing the gap between employee expectations and perceptions increases the likelihood of employee satisfaction, which generally leads to greater employee retention.

A BCO's recruiting message and hiring experience should resonate with candidates

A BCO recruiting message needs to be more than a "we're hiring" advertisement. Ultimately, the message needs to resonate with candidates who would be the best fit with the organization. One technique in drafting such a message is to consider it from the candidates' perspective, with a message that focuses on why working with the organization matters—or should matter—to them. For example, because our organization's audit reports can significantly impact the way the way that California's state agencies and programs operate, our overall recruiting message is "We gather the brightest minds from around the state and nation to make a difference in California Government."

In *Strategies for Effective Branding*, Keever Watts (2014) stresses the importance of addressing the following three needs when recruiting:

- **Autonomy**: In what ways does the organization give employees the freedom to determine how they get work done and with whom they work?
- **Mastery**: In what ways does the organization help its employees continue to master their areas of expertise?
- **Purpose**: In what ways does working for the organization provide employees with a sense of meaning, purpose, or connection to something greater than themselves?

The most successful recruiting messages and marketing campaigns are also tailored to meet candidate expectations. Currently, the candidate pool is primarily composed of the millennial generation. To learn about and understand millennial candidate expectations, BCO recruiters can reference millennial experts, like Lindsey Pollack. Pollack (2015) finds that millennial candidates tend to be attracted to work environments that support flexible schedules, include significant communication and feedback, provide technology to work smarter, and create opportunities for fun along with hard work.

Effective BCO recruiters recognize that not only their recruiting messages but also their hiring processes should model their organizations' core values. For instance, is the hiring process burdensome or overly bureaucratic? Is it timely? Is any part of it automated? Can candidates complete any steps online and at their leisure (e.g., the application or an online examination or assessment)? The BCO hiring process needs to be transparent, credible, and void of any perception that candidates may be hired because of nepotism or connections. Similarly, the hiring questions and assessments should be based on competencies and behaviors required of a candidate to be successful in the position. Further, BCO recruiters need to understand and effectively communicate the hiring process steps to candidates so that they can best prepare for each step.

BCO representatives should also communicate to candidates the hiring process results in a timely manner. BCO recruiters should appreciate that for many candidates, accepting an employment offer is one of the biggest decisions that they will have made at that point in their lives.

A recruiter must appreciate the BCO's brand

Recruiters must truly understand their BCOs' brands before they recruit others to join their organizations. Many recruiters base their personal perceptions of their BCOs' brands on their experiences working with the organizations or on the content of television commercials, social media, and BCO brochures. However, recruiters should confirm whether their perceptions match those of candidates. I recommend that recruiters survey (formally or informally) newer colleagues, career services directors, counselors, faculty, and students for their input and perceptions about BCOs' brands. The recruiters can then compare these individuals' perceptions to those of seasoned colleagues and to the informational materials the BCOs make available to candidates.

The message in the informational materials in particular should be current, authentic, and consistent with candidates' perceptions of a BCO's brand. If inconsistencies exist, it's possible that the materials are dated or that there is a disconnect in how the BCO leadership brands itself and how candidates and others perceive it. Such instances might warrant deeper analysis, including additional surveys and focus groups to address the gap between expectations and perception.

When an organization's brand hinges on the public's perceived trust, it is imperative that the organization takes the necessary measures to protect the brand. For example, in our organization's recruiting materials, the State Auditor describes "Who We Are" as follows:

The California State Auditor leads the way in providing truthful, balanced, and unbiased information to the California State Legislature. We help elected leaders and state agencies improve public services and use taxpayer's money in the most effective ways possible. Our audits and reviews result in accurate and dependable information that helps to clarify issues, pose corrective action for problems, and bring more accountability to government programs. We pride ourselves on proposing innovative solutions to problems that are identified by our work so State agencies can better serve the public of California.

This message makes clear that credibility is paramount to our organization's brand. To protect that brand, our organization has established many layers of quality control to ensure that our report findings are substantiated and add value to the agencies and programs we audit.

The best example I know in which an organization restored public trust and confidence in its brand involves Johnson & Johnson, the makers of Tylenol. In 1982, someone tampered with Tylenol bottles in Chicago, lacing the capsules with potassium cyanide and killing seven people. Johnson & Johnson responded by quickly halting production, warning hospitals, and issuing a nationwide recall of over $100 million worth of Tylenol products. To further restore public trust and confidence, Johnson & Johnson's CEO, James Burke, personally led a committee to produce tamper-proof packaging. Moreover, when Johnson & Johnson relaunched Tylenol capsules, it distributed 40 million $2.50 coupons to recompense consumers for capsules they may have thrown away. Soon after, Tylenol had 30 percent of the market again—close to its pre-incident market share (Brown, 2012).

In discussing Johnson & Johnson's actions, Burke emphasized the value of its credo, which states that the company is responsible first to its customers, then to its employees, the community and the stockholders, in that order. "The credo is all about the consumer," Burke said. According to Burke, "the credo made it very clear [at the time of the seven deaths] exactly what we were all about. It gave me the ammunition I needed to persuade shareholders and others to spend the $100 million on the recall. The credo helped sell it."

For the BCO recruiter, James Burke's lesson is that in order for a recruiting message to be regarded as credible, it needs to be consistent with an organization's values. It also needs to accurately depict the BCO's work product, reputation, environment, and experience.

What it takes to "win the war"

Effective BCO recruiters recognize the value of relationships and foster authentic partnerships with many campus college representatives. They convey credible recruiting messages that accurately depict their organizations and encompass their positions' opportunities and challenges. Successful BCO recruiters are also mindful of the candidate experience during the recruiting and hiring processes. Further, the recruiters adopt practices and technology that are current and that best attract and accommodate talented candidates. Ultimately, effective BCO recruiters are driven by their relationships with both the candidates and the college representatives rather than by hiring metrics. Their success in hiring talented candidates is the outcome of the relationships themselves.

References:

Huntford, R. *(1985)*. Shackleton. London: Hodder & Stoughton.

David Brown, Washington Post, October 1, 2012

Time Magazine, Knowledge@Wharton, October 5, 2012

Watts, S. K. (July 2014) Strategies for Effective Branding: Part 1. NACE: Spotlight for Recruiting Professionals.

Making the Old New: Innovative Ways to Rebrand an Established Firm as Sexy

Ren Herring

What does it mean for students to perceive a company as sexy? The meaning may be different to each individual, but for the sake of this article the word "sexy" will represent the meaning behind the words cool, innovative, new, and trendy, but most of all <u>different</u> and how a firm represents that uniqueness.

Contrary to popular belief, differentiation in the campus recruitment marketplace is not about a firm's or company's prestige, services rendered, or clientele served. In today's environment and in the eyes of potential campus candidates, differentiation is about a firm's culture, community, and the opportunity for individuals to grow their own ways. For start-ups and tech firms this is very much a common theme, however, for established companies that have been around for centuries or even a few decades it has become difficult to navigate the campus recruitment landscape against a culture of newer sexy competitors.

For an established company to win the war on talent, the recruiter needs to be an innovative leader that will change the game and be able to communicate why his/her firm is sexy and unique. In essence, the recruiter becomes the firm's cultural warrior and is responsible for developing a multi-step plan that ensures candidates see the represented firm as sexy. The following sections outline a five-step plan on how to make an established brand sexy and relevant in a competitive marketplace.

Step One: Discover sexy

It is the recruiter's responsibility to discover how to differentiate the brand on campus through a multi-step, multi-faceted process that takes time, effort, and innovation. Individualizing an established brand in the eyes of college students will require the discovery of a vision and the ability to put that vision into action. First and foremost, before one gets started, it's important to note that every college campus has its own unique culture and that there is no one-step approach to discovering sexy. Finding sexy will require individualization for each campus. However, regardless of the campus, there are two important questions that must be solved in order for a recruiter to accurately discover what is sexy about his/her firm:

1. What are the current trends that define sexy to students?
2. What is outdated and no longer sexy?

As a recruiter at an established firm, it is important to constantly update your approach because like most cultural phenomena, sexy is in a constant state of evolution. To discover what sexy is, it is suggested to implement a mixed-methods research approach that focuses both on qualitative and quantitative research.

Following are a few suggestions:

- For the qualitative research portion, it is suggested that a recruiter holds focus groups with key target demographics such as:
  - Recent graduates who have joined the firm in the past year. These candidates will provide a common and specific answer/theme as to why they accepted offers, where the recruitment process was strong, and where it needs to be improved.
  - Candidates who interviewed for the firm and received offers, but declined them. These candidates will provide information about the firm's weaknesses, but more important where they did not connect or identify with the firm during the recruitment process.
  - Newly elected student leaders who are eager to implement change. Each year a new set of student leaders takes on leadership roles with agendas filled with goals, change, and innovation. It is recommended that recruiters work early-on with these newly elected leaders to find out what their goals are and how they want to shape their club's future. The recruiter should offer to work with the newly elected student leaders to create new programming that implements their

ideas. It shows that the represented firm is cutting-edge, open to ideas, and willing to foster personal growth. Furthermore, it provides the recruiter with the ability to see the process through the candidates' eyes.

- For the quantitative research portion, it is suggested that the recruiter send online surveys to candidates involved in the different steps of the process. Surveys should be multiple choice with some open-ended text-entry questions. It is recommended that you send surreys to candidates who applied but did not receive interviews; those who received interviews, but not offers; and those who received offers.

  o Example questions include:
    o What most attracted you to the firm?
    o How did you hear about the opportunity?
    o Were there any influential individuals that motivated you to apply?
    o What is your favorite aspect of the firm?
    o How can we improve the process for next year's candidates?

Step Two: Make sexy personal and consistent

The next step in the process is perhaps the most difficult as the recruiter must navigate and condense multiple storylines into a consistent message. It becomes particularly difficult because the message must translate at both an individual level and the group level as many recruitment events involve multiple candidates. Through the "Discover Sexy" research examples outlined in step one, the recruiter should have identified three-to-five overarching examples of what differentiates his/her firm. Examples may include flexible work schedules, personal development opportunities, and diversity. It is now time to turn these examples into talking points and relate them to how an established firm is actually cutting-edge and leading the industry in these particular examples. A good recruiter will weave the differentiators into every candidate conversation and presentation by providing personal examples and ensuring that the entire team is on message and portraying the firm as sexy. An even better recruiter will host roundtables and conversations where students can meet with client service staff and alumni to hear several personal narratives about how these differentiators made an impact in different ways.

Step Three: Restructure your budget to accommodate sexy

Regardless of opportunity, there will always be several restraints a recruiter must overcome. One of the most important is the ability to balance a budget to ensure maximum exposure to the firm in a smart and strategic way. Before each semester, the recruiter should sit down and separate the budget into three distinct areas that forecast spending:

1. Travel and accommodations for the client service team
2. Mandatory recruiting events such as on-campus interviews, receptions, career-fairs, & corporate presentations
3. Sexy fund

The sexy fund is where innovation comes into play and will require creative work and leadership on behalf of the recruiter beyond the traditional mandatory recruitment events. Each event held with sexy funds should be strategic and address specific goals that are discovered in steps one and two. This may mean reestablishing, tweaking, or axing traditions, approaching events in a new way, and working with student leaders at the grassroots level to develop specific events that target the intended audience. It is advised that all sexy fund events have a professional development takeaway for the candidates. These events should never be the average firm's/company's 101 presentation with a PowerPoint. They should be specific and address themes such as strategic thinking, case walk-throughs, balancing budgets, how to improve strengths and weaknesses, learning new skills, etc. Over time and with practice, sexy fund events will become easier and easier as students and client service members of the recruitment team become more involved. By involving students and client service staff in the development of events, the recruiter is providing personal growth opportunities and empowering the team to work harder and smarter. In turn, they too will provide insight and ideas on how to create more sexy events that align with the personal and consistent sexy message that was created in step two. At this point in the process, students will begin viewing the established firm as sexy in a way that they did not previously.

Step Four: Be brave, be bold, and expect failure

There are many advantages for recruiters that represent an established brand, however there are also many challenges. Transforming an established brand into a sexy brand is not and will not be easy. There will be times during the transformation period that are difficult and will result in failure. However, failure is part of the sexy growing process and transformation cannot take place unless the recruiter is willing to be brave, bold, and courageous. Failure in many ways, is only the start of sexy success. If an idea to achieve sexy doesn't work, it doesn't mean that it is bad – it most likely means that it needs to be refined, retuned, and tried again. Following are a few of examples on how to best navigate potential failure when rolling-out a new project:

- Disregard fear, let go of ego, and embrace and implement ideas of non-recruiters.

- When rolling out a new project, workshop, or competition, inform the participating candidates that the event is a pilot and that constructive feedback is appreciated.

- Hold a feedback session at the end of each new sexy event before ending it and then implement the feedback and try the event on a new audience.

- Remember that transformation of an established brand to a sexy brand is 100% about curated events and challenging candidates through personal growth.

- Remember that sexy is never about giveaways, ambiance, fancy dinners, or courting a candidate. All competitors are capable of wining and dining candidates and are able to provide unique material items. If you can touch it, it is not a differentiator.

Step Five: Refine, retune, and roll-out sexy!

The final step in the process is to roll-out sexy with confidence and ease. Steps one through four should take an academic year to complete and by the time step five is reached, the recruiter should have had a transformative experience that not only enhances and changes the firm's brand on campus, but the recruiter's personal brand as well. Through the process of enhancing an established brand into sexy, the recruiter will have impacted many students on campus. Former and current interns, student leaders, and those involved

---

in pilots will all now view the established firm as sexy and begin to spread the word on campus. This is the pivotal moment known as the roll-out, in which success is reached as college students are highly responsive to their environmental circumstances and often times their career ambitions are impacted by fellow students. Once the brand is defined as sexy and has reached roll-out status, it is important to constantly update and create new programming and events to stay competitive.

Conclusion: A sexy brand is personal, confident, and approachable

Once the recruiter has established the firm as a differentiated and sexy brand that focuses on personal and professional development of potential candidates – the interest on campus, quality of candidates, and talent pipeline will all increase significantly. The transformation of how the brand is interpreted will never be tangible or easy to notice, which is why the recruiter must grow confident with ambiguity and the implementation of new ideas. The gradual change that this multi-step plan outlines will be marked a success when candidates communicate among each other about the brand, its initiatives, and its culture when the recruiter is not present.

As a recruiter that has reestablished the way in which an established brand is interpreted on campus, I leave three pieces of advice for new recruiters implementing sexy. Make the journey personal, be confident throughout, and always be approachable and open to new ideas. If these three pieces of advice are followed, making an established brand sexy will occur holistically.

Recruiting in the U.K: The Jaguar Land Rover Experience

Graham Thompsett

Background

Jaguar Land Rover (JLR) has delivered tremendous growth that has seen us invest heavily in our business in recent years. Our continued success lies in our ability to deliver the next generation of ever more advanced, desirable but sustainable products that delight and excite our customers in over 170 countries worldwide. We can only do this if we attract, develop and retain the best talent to deliver our ambitious plans. We must continue to recruit the next generation of innovators who will shape the future of our company and the wider industry.

In just over 6 years we have demonstrated our commitment by investing in people – our most important asset. We have grown from an organisation with 9,000 employees in 2009 to over 40,000 globally in 2016. Investment in the numbers of graduates and undergraduate placement students into the business has been significant with just less than 2,000 graduates and 850 undergraduate placement students joining us on their journeys into their careers that are making a real contribution.

Attraction

Unlike the US, who has always funded their degrees, investment for a degree is a relatively new in the UK. Evidence shows that this investment has had an influence on the human behaviour of an undergraduate in deciding where they study and live, both during, and after their degree. For example, those that decide to study in London can expect to have the greatest investment (or debt) with tuition fees and high living costs; however, they then have a greater inclination to remain in the Capital where salaries and opportunities are perceived to be most competitive. In contrast, people born in Scotland may choose to study there as their degree will be funded by Government.

This personal investment has also impacted on how undergraduates approach the job markets with 77% admitting to job hunting prior to their final year.

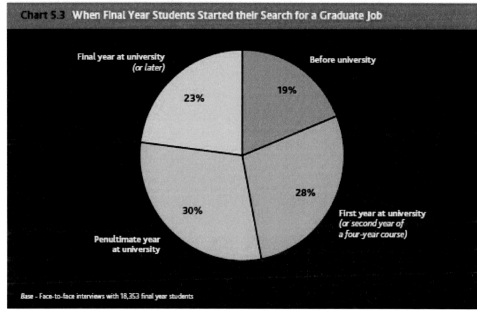

Chart 5.3 When Final Year Students Started their Search for a Graduate Job

Final year at university (or later) — 23%

Before university — 19%

First year at university (or second year of a four-year course) — 28%

Penultimate year at university — 30%

Base - Face-to-face interviews with 18,353 final year students

SOURCE: UK Graduate Careers Survey 2006-2016

As a prospective employer, the challenge is that we need to have a highly effective attraction plan that is both traditional and strategic. It needs to include applicants from first to final year at the same time as informing and promoting the numerous opportunities JLR has to offer. We need to endorse:

- Learning – structured, mentoring, personal development plans, professional accreditation etc.
- Career development – both locally and globally
- Work-life balance

Traditional approach

In support of traditional methods, a recent UK Graduate Careers Survey demonstrated the continued importance of the careers service; graduate websites, brochures and careers fairs and the roles they play in strengthening a recruitment message.

University Careers Service

The university careers service in the UK plays a vital role in supporting and advising undergraduates. 95% of final year undergraduates surveyed confirm they used their local careers service whilst seeking advice on the prospective graduate vacancies and organisations.

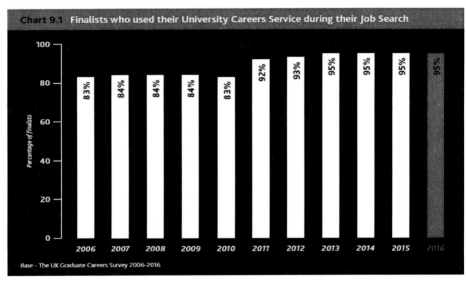

Chart 9.1 Finalists who used their University Careers Service during their Job Search

Base – The UK Graduate Careers Survey 2006-2016

SOURCE: UK Graduate Careers Survey 2006-2016

At JLR we have University Campus Teams associated with 30 Universities across the UK and Ireland. Volunteers from the business support the campus teams and represent our Engineering & Corporate functions. The JLR volunteers are usually alumni of the associated university but this is not essential. The teams collaborate with the careers service and key activities include:

- Ensuring information on JLR is up to date and relevant across the university
- Regularly contacting careers advisers to ensure they are aware of JLR's recruitment plans i.e. open for applications/closing dates
- Discussing annual plans to ensure JLR get the best location at a careers event or book the best slots for skills training workshops or employer presentations
- Advertising opportunities via careers service email or societies with social

126

media sites e.g. Engineering Society Twitter or Facebook – often this communication is targeted and it can have an excellent return at a very low cost

- Obtaining introductions to specific academic departments thus allowing a depth of knowledge and quality relationship with academics and students on particular courses with niche skills e.g. Design, Electrical Engineering etc.

Graduate Websites

Research also shows that graduate websites continue to be the most widely-used recruitment promotion during the employment search. There are several ways that recruiters can ensure their websites are effective:

- locate your graduate recruitment site within your organisation's main website – don't create another unique URL
- provide substantial information that is well organised and easy to browse
- ensure you include location and salary
- make the application process visible and user friendly
- include images
- avoid internal jargon
- consider that a high percentage of users will not be in their final year so try and provide information for all – undergraduates, short term programmes, work experience etc.

Recent feedback on JLR website

Jaguar Land Rover

Agency - **Pink Squid**   *Website -* jaguarlandrovercareers.com/jlr-roles/future-talent

Summary - Finalists praised the structure of the site, and felt that the design was very modern, engaging and easy to digest.

Comments - "Very appealing and attractive to the user".

"Format and images are exciting and make you want to stay on the site. It has all the information needed".

SOURCE: UK Graduate Careers Survey 2006-2016

Strategic focus

The HR vision and strategic plan is designed to support the long-term goals to develop a sustainable business.

Undergraduate Conversions

Although the number of graduates hired is higher than undergraduates the reality has been that the demand for graduates in our business has been a stable requirement year on year. This is compared to the demand for undergraduates which has experienced significant growth. There are multiple benefits to JLR of investing in undergraduate placements:

- fantastic way to promote JLR as an employer with several future talent programmes
- an opportunity to recruit motivated individuals in a reasonably inexpensive way
- the knowledge that JLR gains about the person - their motivation, work ethic and future plans allows us to create a strong pipeline for our graduate programmes – they are the future
- undergraduates who have JLR experience can return to university as brand ambassadors to further strengthen the JLR communications
- the future recruitment of a graduate who is engaged and ready to start work with prior knowledge of the business and all it can offer

A real proven example of the benefit is that 49% of those that were offered a graduate role in 2016 had previously completed one or more undergraduate placements with the business.

Women in Engineering

Improving the gender balance is a priority for JLR and to support our strategy to employ more women JLR has developed strong programmes and partnerships with the Women in Engineering Society (WES), Engineering Network for Women (12th year) and the Women in Engineering Sponsorship Scheme which offers a bursary for female undergraduates studying engineering.

Each programme/partnership demonstrates our commitment to increasing the number of women in our business and permits us to engage with a broad range of female talent in different ways – perhaps the sponsorship of an event, managing and judging a project relevant to our business, recognition awards for outstanding contribution/special project etc.

We host specific Women in Engineering undergraduate and graduate recruitment events in addition to the work delivered by the campus teams. Popular and well supported, these events allow us to demonstrate the success of the females we already employ who are committed to promoting JLR and encouraging further talent to apply to our recruitment programmes. In fact, the current winner of the IET (Institute of Engineering and Technology) Young Woman Engineer of the Year made her initial application to JLR following her attendance at one of these events, completed 2 undergraduate summer placements, was awarded a bursary and took employment on graduation with us.

In 2016 34% of graduate offers were made to women - a 7% year on year increase.

Degree Apprenticeships

In the UK, the growth in opportunities and the increasing popularity to complete a degree apprenticeship is important to JLR's strategic plans.

The degree apprenticeship scheme allows those who have successfully completed their A Levels, usually at the age of 18, (or BTEC Level 3 equivalent) to start training/working. The UK Government has placed great emphasis on apprenticeship opportunities and this, coupled with a noted increase in companies offering opportunities in the school leaver space, has definitely seen a shift downward in an entry level to an employer. In addition, the media have chosen to highlight the popularity of apprenticeship positions as opposed to attending university and the associated financial burden.

In JLR we offer a degree apprenticeship programme which, through a blended approach of learning and on the job responsibility, supports an apprentice to obtain a degree at the end of a six-year programme. We have seen a considerable increase in the number of applications received for our apprenticeship programmes. In part, we assume that the financial investment of tuition fees, in addition to living expenses, means that apprenticeship programmes are increasing in appeal to students and also their parents. Another reason why degree apprenticeships might be so popular is it can give the opportunity to a student to obtain a degree in a way that might not otherwise be available. Social mobility studies continue to highlight the challenges faced by individuals from lower income families or deprived areas.

This salaried apprenticeship programme can present an opportunity to acquire a degree with little or no financial investment on their part.

JLR has seen the number of vacancies increase from 49 in 2012 to 140 in 2016 – a growth of 286%. If this trend continues to rise, with us and other companies, it could impact both the numbers opting to attend university as well as the numbers we recruit into our graduate and undergraduate programmes. However, central to our business plans will be the impact of the apprentice levy as proposed by the Government. The apprentice levy will be applied to all industries in the UK with a wage bill of £3 million and will come into force in April 2017. Funding will be generated at a rate of 0.5% of an employer's wage bill and supports the Government's commitment to delivering 3 million apprenticeships by 2020 – a 35% increase over the 2.2 million apprenticeships delivered in the last Parliament. The levy is intended to provide the funding and incentives to help deliver this commitment. JLR's position on this is not yet clear.

Global

Although we have not yet designed our global graduate recruitment programme we have started our journey by engaging an RPO (Recruitment Process Outsource) that has a global network/capability platform.

We expect this partnership will allow us to be flexible in our approach and further increase our knowledge of how we can enhance our success in the UK and advance our presence in Europe and beyond.

Application process

The expectation that technology supports the application process is without question. Most organisations have applicant tracking systems (ATS) more commonly known as on-line application forms. The best of these systems manages multiple programmes or vacancies and the end to end recruitment requirements from job analysis to offer. In addition to greater efficiencies, the benefits of having the right ATS in place is it allows employers to do much more than data collection, for example, it can protect an employer from risk in terms of data protection, equal opportunity or discrimination legislation.

Within JLR our ATS supports on-line application, candidate communication and the administration of compulsory situational judgement tests and on-line psychometric tests.

Situation Judgement Tests (SJT)

All graduates and undergraduates who apply to JLR will complete an application form and situational judgement test.

Unlike other psychological tests our SJT is not an "off the shelf" product but it has been designed as a bespoke tool which is tailor made to reflect the requirements of JLR. The candidate will be sent a link from the ATS and they are presented with a series of video clips containing some background information which they are asked to consider. They are presented with realistic, hypothetical scenarios and they are required to identify the most appropriate response or rate/rank the response in an order they think is most effective.

There is no time limit for this assessment but it is likely to take candidates 20 minutes to complete.

Example of an SJT scenario

This fair process is the first filter in the JLR application for graduate and undergraduates.

On-line Psychometric Tests

Following the successful completion of the SJT candidates will then be invited to complete three on-line psychometric tests. Many employers use aptitude assessments as part of their assessment process as research has shown that they are powerful predictors of performance at work.

JLR request that graduates and undergraduates complete numerical, verbal and diagrammatical tests. These are timed however, unlike SJT, candidates can complete time practice questions in advance.

An example of a Diagrammatical Test

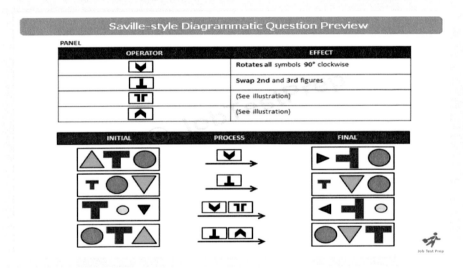

This test is a second filter in JLR's process.

Assessment Centres

Once the on-line tests are complete the next stage would be an invitation to an assessment centre relevant to the desired programme.

Whilst HR provide the assessment material and facilitate it is the responsibility of the business to assess and decide who they are going to recruit into their business. At present, this is the first and only opportunity for the candidate to meet business representative and vice versa.

ATS Reporting

A further benefit of an ATS is the reporting functionality. In JLR we receive a "dashboard" that permits us to review key performance indicators. Examples are:

- Diversity monitoring – male vs. female / British, Black, Asian, and Minority Ethnic (BAME)
- Number of applications vs. University performance – how many applications do we receive through to successful offer
- Functional appeal – who is the most popular where do we need to focus our investment e.g. Engineering

Future

Compulsory to the continued success of our graduate and undergraduate programmes is the research and development of the following projects:

- Why do we recruit graduates – what will they do in the future? when will they add value?
- Global – define what we mean by this as there can be many interpretations
- Virtual World – utilise technology to give the candidate a better JLR experience. Provide a visual of our places of work, business led advice in a practical way.

Challenges

We live in an world where business is changing all the time and the automotive industry is no exception in experiencing transformation. In JLR we face challenges in many if not all of the areas below:

- demand and pace of changing technologies – more than a car but a mobility solution
- non-traditional competition e.g. Google's driverless car
- the global economy

- trade barriers legislation
- enviromental and resource challenges
- consumer demands – shorter lead times
- changing nature of cities – urbanisation
- changing consumer profile – car ownership vs. leasing vs. hiring by the day or even hour
- rumours – impacting reputation

JLR will future-proof its business and change from being an automotive manufacturer to considering all possible ways to being a premium mobilty provider.

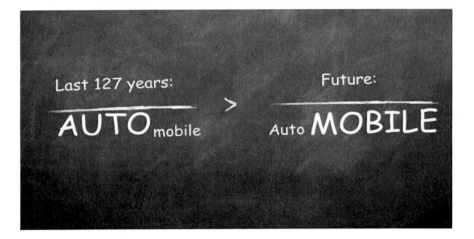

Notwithstanding the challenges facing JLR as a business, we need to ensure we meet the changing "demands" of our future graduate and undergraduates. Research shows that the most important factors in deciding on what companies to apply to and where to accept an offer of employment are:

- content of work
- training and development
- reputation of organisation
- work-life balance

In short the graduate world will continue to change at a quicker pace than most businesses can cope with.

Table 7.12 Job Hunters views on Different Factors when Deciding which Employers to Apply to	Very Important %	Quite Important %	Not Important %
Content of work	61	35	4
Quality of training & development programme	60	36	4
Overall reputation of the organisation	52	43	5
Where the jobs are located	52	38	10
Work-life balance	44	46	10
Culture of the organisation	43	46	11
Starting salary & additional benefits	41	48	11
Quality of staff already working for the organisation	39	50	11
Organisation's business performance and business success	38	49	13
Potential to work for the organisation long-term	35	50	15
Employer is a well-known organisation	29	48	23
Opportunity to work overseas	29	40	31
Employer's 'corporate social responsibility' record	27	50	23
Number of graduate jobs available at employer	24	46	30

Base - Face-to-face interviews with 18,353 final year students

SOURCE: UK Graduate Careers Survey 2006-2016

In JLR we offer roles that have real responsibility, we have comprehensive training & development programmes that support recognised professional accreditation, we are cognisant of the need for career progression and have an organised graduate network in place and proactive in supporting a good work-life balance.

Conclusion

Our successful brand, enviable graduate and undergraduate schemes, has a great reputation that many other organisations envy and that we are immensely proud of. Evidence that our collaboration works is the picture below which introduces you to the apprentices and graduates who joined us in September 2015.

NOTE

* UK Graduate Careers Survey 2016 is based on face-to-face interviews with 18,353 final year students from the 'Class of 2016' studying at thirty leading universities in the UK, carried out in February 2016. It is one of the largest independent surveys of the country's top finalists ever conducted and the sample includes a fifth of students graduating in the summer of 2016.

How Can an Employer Become a Career Center MVP?

Diana Gruverman

No rest for the weary

There are many things a campus recruiting team lead has to do to prepare before heading to campus to begin the hectic schedule of the fall and spring recruiting seasons. Start early even though you are exhausted from orienting your new class of interns. The creation of to do lists begin in July, after the interns are settled in and before the full-time class arrives for training. The list of tasks is formidable. It includes a strategic review of headcount needs, which requires collaboration with business heads. Assess the preliminary successes and failures of the prior year's school campaign. Then, revise marketing and branding materials, update job descriptions, and create budget projections. At the same time, the busy work of reserving tables at career fairs, booking interview rooms, and making other various campus connections complete the initial tasks. If all of this is done correctly, an organization that offers career potential has positioned itself as an employer of choice among target college students. You will increase visibility over the prior year, yield higher event attendance, garner more job applicants, and convert higher quality hires.

Employers aim to present a positive image to students that is enticing: a clean table cloth, a brightly colored banner, trendy SWAG, or the newest gadget. However, have you explored how the brand and image is perceived by students? Don't assume you have all the answers. Collaboration is important in higher education. It feels different than collaboration within a corporate setting, perhaps because of the shared goal of creating a meaningful experience for students while they are in school, and guiding them towards the end goal of graduating with a full-time job. At most schools, administrators work together, and it is important to gain the support of all key stakeholders: students, career centers, administrators, deans, faculty, alumni, and parents. It is also important to communicate to all of them so your message on campus is consistent. By building strong relationships with frequent communications, and by keeping the career center apprised of your activity across campus, you will increase your visibility and avoid duplicate and competing events.

As a campus recruiting professional with over 15 years of experience, I bring a unique perspective to creating a path to becoming an MVP on campus. Recently, I transitioned to a new role as the Americas Campus Recruiting Team Lead at a large, multi-national insurance company. We are a small team with ambitious goals. I was brought in to develop a new way of thinking about our recruitment process to make insurance sound sexy to a 20-year old. However, prior to joining the risk-averse, high tech world of insurance (yes, I said high tech: think drones to evaluate property damage, assessing the risk of driverless cars, and endless safety measures offered by wearable devices), I started my career at the NYU Wasserman Center for Career Development, where I was trained as a career coach and an employer engagement strategist. Through the dot com bubble burst and the great recession, my team and I worked tirelessly to keep employers engaged and connected with our students to yield solid career outcomes. I describe some of these simple, low cost or no cost strategies below.

You don't have to have an open requisition to visit campus

The recruiting landscape is changing, and it is no longer just about filling current headcount. As a recruiter, it is important to keep talented candidates in the pipeline. Some first and second year students may not be ready to think about a "career," but they may have heard from a friend or family member that creating a resume is important. Ask your favorite career center if you can help review resumes (review their resume guidelines before you meet with students). This is a great way to get to know students without the pressure of a job interview. Learn about their background and experiences while providing professional tips and guidance. Not only will you meet interesting candidates, but you will also gain brand recognition through word of mouth. If you are feeling generous, take a group of students out to a local coffee shop and conduct the resume reviews there. Make sure to coordinate with the career center first to avoid competing events.

Similarly, mock interviews are another way to get in front of talent without "recruiting." While I think recruiters and career coaches agree that a mock interview should be required, unfortunately, many career centers do not have the capacity to provide a mock interview to every student who wants one. Offer your expertise by spending an afternoon conducting mock interviews on campus. You will be amazed at how fulfilling it is to see the transition from the first question to the last answer.

There are many other ways to spend time on campus in a non-recruiting capacity. Offer to facilitate a workshop. Most career centers offer standardized workshops on topics such as Resume Writing, Interview Skills, Job Search, and Networking. Pick a topic you are comfortable to present on your own, or team up with a career coach to deliver the content. Utilizing the career center's social media platforms is another way to tap into your target candidate pool. Ask your campus contacts how you can provide content in addition to marketing your events through these channels.

Preparation goes beyond the campus recruiting team

How much consideration do you give to those who represent your organization on campus? As a recruiter, you expect students to be prepared to meet you. Candidates should know basic information about your organization, the industry, and relevant current events. Similarly, you should be prepared to meet the candidates. Learn which majors are relevant and which classes are taught. Identify appropriate clubs so they stand out on a resume. If the school is in an urban setting, it is more common to see academic year internships. Academic year internships are often less common at suburban schools. Know if you are comparing apples to apples.

It is a safe assumption that most recruiting teams begin each season with a common set of talking points (if you are not already doing this, please start). This might include a summary of the summer intern and analyst training programs, a list of the businesses you recruit for, interesting new products, highlights of philanthropy, interesting diversity statistics, along with a few public affairs bullet points. Also, consider highlighting school-specific information at each campus, such as the number of intern and full-time hires from the previous season and upcoming interview and event dates. These same talking points should be provided to anyone who represents your brand on campus, from alumni to senior speakers, whether it is at a career fair, an interview, or an information session.

From my experience, two of the most important questions that everyone should be able to answer are:

1. Do you hire students who require sponsorship to legally work in the U.S.?
2. Do you hire graduate students?

These are often uncomfortable questions to answer, but they are important qualifications that all candidates and representatives should understand. To avoid bouncing candidates between recruiters, alumni, and career coaches, provide clear and consistent information about these and other job applicant facts.

Many organizations use former interns as "campus ambassadors" when they return to campus. Hold a training for these interns in September, and provide them with the talking points too. Encourage them to spread the word about the exciting summer internship experience they had. Ask them to share information through social media platforms. Invite them to join you at events, such as career fairs or information sessions. They can also serve as greeters during your on-campus interviews. If you can manage it, consider paying your campus ambassadors.

Mutual respect

What would an interviewer think of a candidate who sent texts or emails during the interview? The candidate would probably not receive positive feedback. Conversely, what would a candidate think of an interviewer who sent texts or emails during an interview? The candidate would be turned off, and this will immediately be shared with peers and the career center. Remind all interviewers to put away the phone during an interview.

Encourage all representatives to be respectful when they visit campus. Remember, the career center is there to make sure things run smoothly during the interview day, not to make sure things run smoothly for an unrelated business meeting. With advanced notice, a career center may be able to open early, remain open late, or reserve a conference room, but these exceptions should be politely made in advance, and the career center should not be viewed as a personal assistant for printing tons of documents unrelated to the interview process or event.

Listen to your current interns and new campus hires

By leveraging the experiences and opinions of summer interns and recent full-time hires, you can gain insight into your target audience, and further refine your campus recruiting strategy. I previously mentioned the idea of a campus ambassador—a former summer intern who is trained to talk about his or her recruiting and summer internship experience. You can recruit these ambassadors during the summer from your high potential interns.

Identify a cross section of summer interns or recent hires and conduct one or more focus groups. The moderator should ask questions about the following:

- job application process
- interview
- onboarding
- orientation and training
- performance feedback
- overall communication
- school specific information

Expect a range of both positive and negative responses. Some feedback will be very specific and, hopefully, easy to implement. Some feedback will be general and more difficult to address. Understanding the experiences and ideas of your new hires is how you will stay fresh, and it can potentially help you recognize misconceptions about your industry.

Alumni are your golden tickets

Alumni are often an underutilized resource within campus recruiting, and, while they can be used in many ways, I have outlined a few below that can help you achieve solid recruiting results. Begin by identifying alumni within your organization who are top performers in a variety of departments and who are passionate about their undergrad or graduate alma mater. Once you have selected the alumni, ask them to contribute their time by:

- Screening resumes: train alumni how to review resumes and allow them to review the resume bundle from their school. Since they know the courses and faculty, they can help identify top performers.

- Conducting interviews: train alumni to interview. The students will relate to the alumni since they have a common history.

- Attending a career fair: recent graduates are perfect for noticing familiar faces in the crowd and inviting them to visit your table.

- Presenting welcome remarks: this is a nice honor for an alumnus who has demonstrated success within your organization. Remarks can be made to candidates at on-campus or on-site recruiting events, as well as to new hires as they enter your organization.

It is sometimes challenging to identify all alumni of a particular school within your organization. LinkedIn makes this easier. You can also connect with the alumni or development office at your target schools for a list of alumni who are employed within your organization.

Don't be lazy

If you aren't sure where to begin, identify your key college partners, and ask the career center for guidance. Since the partnership should be mutually beneficial, ask what you can do to support the achievement of the career center's goals. Students develop strong, personal relationships with their career coaches over many years. Students go to the career center first when they encounter a problem during the recruiting process: managing exploding offers, interpreting job offers, and reporting questionable interview practices. However, students also provide positive feedback too: events they found unique and engaging, dynamic speakers, and technology driven innovation. This is where career development professionals gain valuable insight into how to build a successful employer brand on campus. If you leverage your relationship carefully, you can benefit from this wealth of knowledge.

The recruiting landscape is changing because the candidates are changing. What works in urban setting with countless cheese steaks may not work in a sprawling campus with countless palm trees. Recruiters are trying to stay one step ahead of the candidates, and it is important to partner with career centers to remain relevant. Some recruiters are setting the pace, and others are playing catch up. Which one do you want to be?

Maximizing the Career Services Relationship

Trudy Steinfeld and Emanuel Contomanolis

The last decade has been marked by a vast amount of change in the campus-based recruiting of college educated talent. Recruiting organizations are lean and often under-staffed; new technologies and approaches constantly shift hiring strategies and processes; metric driven data analytics increasingly drive decisions; recruiting cycles for intern and graduating student hires have become compressed and have started earlier than ever before; campus recruiters and university relations teams rotate through assignments making stability and consistency challenging; and, of course, competition for talent has never been more fierce.

Success under these challenging circumstances demands partnerships and effective collaborations and perhaps the most important of these are with the university's career services organization. It's critical to understand, however, how much has also changed in university career services work. Universities are under fire for ever rising costs and the perceived value for the return on that investment has never been more questioned. Demonstrable positive career outcomes for graduating students have become vital to nearly every institution's brand and value proposition. Despite the significantly increased pressure to demonstrate those outcomes, most offices are still under-staffed and under-resourced. The expectations of students, faculty, institutional administrators, and recruiters for more extensive and customized programs and services have grown dramatically and most often without incremental resources. Many offices are still in the midst of a paradigm shift away from a traditional counseling and career development assessments to engaged and networked communities of diverse students, recruiters, faculty and alumni with a common interest in selected career paths and industries.

There are indeed a great many career services offices that are enormously effective in supporting the work of recruiting organizations. The sheer number and diversity of higher education institutions and programs, however, with their idiosyncratic cultures, procedures, protocols, and systems can make understanding the institutional landscape and determining how to best apply a given recruiting strategy incredibly daunting and frustrating.

Although all these factors create real challenges to establishing what were once considered traditional recruiting relationships, they also create opportunities for innovative and unique types of engagement. In fact, it is precisely because of all of these influences and demands that a strategic approach to establishing effective partnerships with career services is more vital now than ever. An effective partnership between both parties enhances the prestige of career services among students and institutional stakeholders and helps to advance a recruiting employer's brand and hiring success.

There are a number of important considerations in maximizing the relationship with career services organizations:

Begin with recognizing and accepting that every school is different. Don't assume that what works on one campus will work at another. Urban vs. college town, public vs. private, campus climate and culture along with academic program portfolio and student demographics all present challenges and opportunities. Getting to know the institution, its culture and most importantly the areas of power and influence that can help advance your recruiting strategy is essential. A flexible and adaptable strategy that gives you room to adjust always works best. There are numerous examples of companies insisting on a campus recruiting event that just didn't fit the institutional culture, only to be frustrated and disappointed by the outcome. A career service organization can be very helpful in sharing what works, and what doesn't work, with their students and on their campus.

Understand the fundamental "polarities" in our work. Recruiters are trying to narrow the top end of the candidate funnel and career services organizations are often trying to broaden that top end of the funnel since they are motivated first and foremost by creating more potential opportunities for their students. Recruiters love specific referrals and any help they can get in sorting through candidates. Career services staff, on the other hand, are sometimes very reluctant to be perceived by their students as "playing favorites" or are concerned about the implications of their recommendations should things not work out. Recruiters assume, or at the very least hope, that the university can "speak in one voice" and that the various institutional offices all take recruiting efforts seriously and collaborate closely with one another to best serve the recruiting organization's interests and initiatives.

Universities, however, can be very decentralized and the multiple entities (e.g. career services, alumni relations, fundraising and development, research relations, student clubs and organizations, faculty, academic administrators to name but a few) often have differing, and at times conflicting, priorities. Career services organizations often have to navigate a complex organizational landscape that makes what might appear to be a simple request on the part of the recruiter or recruiting organization more difficult than imaginable to honor. These polarities are not necessarily negative - they just needed to be recognized and navigated as effectively as possible.

Work to dispel any semblance of an "us versus them" mentality when it comes to working with career services. Especially for your core schools, bring the career services leadership into your planning process as early as possible, to provide feedback and gain their support. There are some recruiters that don't fully understand or appreciate the complexities of career services work and the long hours that many staff put in with very modest compensation. Take the time to acknowledge their hard work, and discuss with these important partners ways that you can work together effectively to achieve mutual goals, including helping to prepare students and getting more of them into your talent pipeline.

As you have probably experienced, on some campuses career services professionals see themselves essentially as "counselors" and have traditionally left dealings with recruiters to specific staff members tasked with that responsibility. It is critical to your success that you identify staff members "who get it" and want to find ways to partner. You can demonstrate empathy and make the case that becoming familiar with your organization and its hiring goals and being able to discuss available opportunities builds credibility with students, faculty, and other stakeholders on campus. You may also want to seek out other campus stakeholders (e.g. faculty, student clubs and organizations) that want to work with you to ensure you identify students for your internship and full-time opportunities.

Even in a period of economic and political uncertainty, competition for the best and brightest students remains fierce. Most recruiters are under increasing pressure to create earlier talent pipelines, increase internship conversion rates, and create a desirable brand identity on campus. Increasingly this has resulted in employers' targeting first- and second-year undergraduates and accelerating their internship recruiting timelines. Many faculty and career services professionals are troubled by this, and view these "accelerated" timelines as putting undue pressure and stress on young undergraduates. If you want to enlist their support, try to align your efforts with theirs and offer to provide leadership training, mentorship and other resources to gain their trust and cooperation.

Some career centers do seem to have "a one size fits all approach" and don't always consider an employer's brand visibility, industry, size, and specific hiring needs. Traditional campus recruiting efforts such as attending a career fair, holding a campus presentation, or interviewing on campus may not always be the most effective way to drive students to your organization, but some campuses may be challenged to offer other types of engagement strategies. Under these circumstances, positioning your efforts as "easy wins", exploring the mutual benefits of innovative and nontraditional approaches, such as partnering on targeted social media campaigns, planning student meet-ups, supporting leadership and skill development initiatives, may be a more productive strategy that you can build on.

Every recruiting organization should have a clearly defined campus strategy and corresponding activities that reflect the engagement principles outlined here. Consider the following concepts in the actually implementing that strategy at the individual institution level:

1. Develop an intentional plan for campus engagement and partnership development. This should reflect a multi-faceted approach that engages career services and other campus stakeholders. Create buy-in by involving the career services team and key campus partners as early as possible in your discussions and planning.
2. If you have institutional specific metrics such as hiring data, internship conversion rates, number of alumni employed in your organization, offer to share that information with career services. Those insights are highly valued and properly leveraged can aid your efforts over time.
3. Engage your campus partners in assessing the effectiveness of your talent engagement efforts. For example, some employers are questioning the importance of career fair attendance, although at many campuses it

is consistently at the top of the list of how students first engage with employers. Although well intentioned, sometimes employers plan their campus activities in a vacuum without fully understanding the distinct needs and goals of the campuses they work with. This can be accomplished by any combination of focus groups, surveys and targeted conversations with career services leadership and other stakeholders. Once you have the information, it's important to implement strategies that demonstrate your responsiveness to the feedback you received.

4. Make sure to work closely with and strengthen your ties to individual alumni. Many are willing to serve as "recruiting champions" and may be in a position to advocate for your organization to build or expand a recruiting relationship at a target campus. It's important to be thoughtful when engaging alumni, as many are well intentioned, but have their own campus connections and may not be aware of the firm's strategy. Make sure they are part of your overall strategy and planning meetings and feedback loops if appropriate.

5. Whenever possible, visit career offices or set up virtual meetings and always make it a point to talk with the career services team when you are on campus. Use conferences, professional meetings, and social media tools to network and increase your campus recruiting brand exposure.

6. Offer to conduct presentations on specific industry and career options, rather than information sessions specific to your company. Participate in recruiter-in-residence programs; volunteer as a student or alumni mentor; offer to work with students to support career advisement meetings as appropriate with students; serve as a panelist on targeted career programs; and participate in special events, such as dining etiquette training programs.

Each campus recruiting organization is trying hard to differentiate their brand in an increasingly competitive landscape. As you develop and roll out your college relations strategy, it is critical that you build something that is scalable as you create demand and momentum, delivers on what you have promised, remains flexible, adapts to changing conditions, and allows for follow up with your school partners. The benefits to your organization and your recruiting efforts, as well as for your career services and campus partners, are well worth your investment in these important efforts that will help you in identifying, targeting and hiring college talent.

Experience Is the New Swag:
A New Approach to Attracting Gen Y and Gen Z

Lindsey Pollak

Millennials -- the generation born in the 1980s and 1990s, also known as Generation Y -- are unique individuals, but if there's one characteristic almost all of them share, it is that they are digital natives. They grew up comfortable with computers, integrate technology into every aspect of their lives and crave constant connectivity. Generation Z, the generation born in the 2000s and 2010s, will continue this trajectory and will likely use technology and the Internet in ways we can't even fathom yet.

This, however, is not an essay about technology. It is, rather, an essay about the mindset that technology creates. It is a mindset that all of us are becoming accustomed to, but Gen Ys and Gen Zs will possess innately: It is the mindset of having access to almost the entire universe of information, people and opportunities available to us at the touch of a button.

What does this mean? It means we are all really, *really* tough to impress. Perhaps none more so than the high-potential Gen Ys and Gen Zs top companies want to recruit.

This challenge clicked for me when one of my corporate clients said, "I no longer bring water bottles and T-shirts to recruiting events. I bring my CEO." She told me, "Experience is the new swag." Unique in-person experiences are one of the few perks a smartphone cannot provide. It is not surprising, then, that a study by Eventbrite and Harris (1) found that more than three quarters of millennials would choose to spend money on an experience or event over buying a physical product.

As a recruiter, this means you must reconsider every single experience a candidate has with your company. Now more than ever, each experience is a crucial component of that student's overall impression of your organization. Your website, social media accounts, job fairs and job interview are all touch points that will color their impressions and influence their decisions.

And it doesn't stop there. It's important to think about experience once your hires are on the job, too, during their onboarding, training and overall experience, including the day they leave. Since most young people will not work at your organization for the rest of their careers, these early experiences will shade how they view your organization as a potential place to refer friends, a potential client to do business with and perhaps even an experience they would like to have again as a "boomeranging" future re-hire. I know this may sound exhausting (and it certainly can be), but, at the same time, it creates so many more opportunities for employee engagement than we ever had in the past.

Here are three areas where companies should focus on experience:

What experience do your website and social media create?

Can your potential employees find you where they're looking online? When they check out your Facebook, Twitter or Instagram, do they feel you're speaking their language? Are you providing content that's about them (not about you), and offers ways to interact, rather than just talking at them with a commercial? Do they see people like them on your site? Are you keeping up with website trends so their experience with your site doesn't feel five years behind the rest of their Internet browsing? Is your site mobile-friendly?

Steal this best practice:

Companies that win in the online experience game are those that put the camera in the hands of their millennials, or let young employees take over their recruiting Twitter feed. You want your potential employees to hear the voice of millennials in the company and showcase the opportunities you offer for them to contribute.

What experience does your recruiting process create?

One of my favorite perspectives comes from entrepreneur Carey Smith (2015) who has said, "My millennial employees are my greatest recruitment and retention tool." Are you designing your recruitment process to allow your own young talent to be part of the end-to-end experience? If not, you're missing a valuable opportunity, because millennials want to see what their peers are doing to understand if your company is the kind of place they want to be. How can you engage your young employees more throughout your campus recruiting plan?

Steal this best practice:

One-size-fits-all recruiting dinners and company information sessions just don't stand out in Gen Y and Gen Z minds. Digital natives crave something different — something special. Something, yes, they might be proud to share on Instagram. Maybe you can take recruits on a tour of a unique part of your company, such as the R&D lab. One company I know brings in potential recruits for a full day "Super Saturday" where they roll out the (literal) red carpet and allow prospective employees to experience the company and culture. Of course, the bonus is that hiring managers and employees get to "experience" the candidates, too, leading to a better fit for everyone.

What experience does your onboarding create?

It's a cliché that you never get a second chance to make a good first impression, but it rings true at that crucial time when employees first join your company. Fewer than half of companies have a training program in place, and yet lack of adequate training is one of the top reasons new employees leave a company.

Think about your onboarding practices: Do new hires feel part of the team from Day 1? Have you made sure they're able to meet with key executives, and that they have appropriate training in both hard skills and soft skills? Have you considered pairing them with another, slightly more experienced colleague to help them learn those unwritten rules that will allow them to feel like they immediately fit in? Do you encourage them to update their LinkedIn profiles with their new role?

Steal this best practice:

One financial services company makes it a priority for the senior leadership team to meet new hires on their very first week on the job to welcome them and answer questions. What better way to provide a truly unique, memorable exciting experience at a critical moment in a young person's life?

What's the bottom line?

Recruiters have always been aware that they are creating a candidate "experience," so this topic is not new. What is new is that Gen Ys and Gen

Zs are pushing a level of innovation and creativity that will force recruiters to be at the top of their game at every turn from first handshake to offer letter and beyond. I, for one, can't wait to see where this new dynamic takes us all.

References:

Millennials: Fueling the Experience Economy. Retrieved from http://eventbrite-s3.s3.amazonaws.com/marketing/Millennials_Research/Gen_PR_Final.pdf)

Smith, Carey. 5 surprising habits of boomer bosses who get millennials. (2015, May 5). Inc. http://www.inc.com/carey-smith/5-surprising-habits-of-boomer-bosses-who-get-millennials.html

Four Keys to a Successful Internship Program Experience

Caroline Cunningham

Introduction

As a Theater Major at a small liberal arts college in the late 80's, I thought an internship would be a great way to get practical work experience. With my sights set on learning about television production, I identified an internship working for a television show that hosted live stand-up comedy. While the experience was fun and I got to meet some very talented up and coming comedians like Tim Allen and Blake Clark, it was not the intern experience I expected. My duties consisted of making grocery runs to stock the office refrigerator, reconciling the petty cash and holding up the applause meter at the live tapings when the laughter wasn't at the right level. These were certainly not tasks that allowed me to use my education or that gave me a glimpse of what a career in television production could be like. I left this internship laughing but with no further interest in pursuing a career in television.

Just like the company I worked for, many companies lack direction in how to create an outstanding intern experience. A poor experience can be detrimental to a company's image as well as to their intern to full time conversion rate. Conversely, a great experience can boost a company's reputation, improve conversion rates and even deliver free advertising in the form of intern spokespeople. Today's interns Tweet, blog, Pin, post, Snap Chat and Instagram about everything. A great (or not so great) experience will rapidly go viral. By taking the time to implement just a few key principals, companies can ensure a very successful and mutually beneficial intern experience.

Create an environment that promotes reciprocity

Reciprocity is one of the most important intern program principles. Fostering a mutually beneficial relationship is the core to creating a great intern

---

experience. The idea of the company benefiting from the intern is just as important as the intern benefiting from the company as each can learn and grow from each other.

Lucinda Macias, Intern Program Specialist at Chevron Corporation shared Chevron's philosophy on the topic:

"Our intern program is designed to foster an environment that allows for mutual evaluation of future employment. At Chevron, interns are provided with a robust internship experience that adds value to the company and to the intern. We approach the internship as an 8 to 12 week interview. We are able to evaluate the intern and they are able to evaluate us. It's incredibly important to create an experience that not only lets the intern grow and learn but also allows them to see what it would be like to have a long-term career with Chevron. A positive interview outcome may result in a future job opportunity with Chevron which is a win-win for both parties."

"At the beginning of the summer, each intern establishes written performance goals and objectives along with their supervisor. It's important that these are mutually agreed upon, realistic and complimentary to the student's education and course of study. They are also designed to allow the student to build business acumen and learn to navigate in a corporate environment. Many interns are actually given a small capital project or piece of a project to manage. Supervisors get a chance to see how the interns are able to operate and also get the benefit of assistance on critical projects."

Macias went on to say, *"Along with individual projects, Chevron enhances the experience by hosting an annual intern conference. Interns from around the country gather for a full day of networking, hearing from company leaders, exploring the company, building business acumen and learning about possible career paths. Activities like these give the interns a chance to see the big picture and typically result in boosting offer acceptance rates."* Macias commented that Chevron's executives are quick to sign up as speakers. *"They tend to get as much out of it as the interns as there is a sense of energy and excitement that arises when you bring together hundreds of young, talented students for the day."*

Macias finished by sharing that at the end of the internship, each intern delivers a formal presentation to senior leadership. The presentation is an opportunity for each intern to share an overview of his/her project and results as well as for leaders to observe presentation and communication skills. The presentation along with the intern's overall performance goal results contribute to Chevron's decision to extend a returning internship or full time offer.

Provide interns with meaningful work

Providing meaningful work assignments may be the single-most important factor in developing a successful internship experience. Both students and employers need to gauge how well they are suited to each other, and that requires providing the student with "real" work and projects, not just menial tasks such as I was given in my television production internship. (NACE 2013) Work assignments should allow the intern to take their academic experience and apply it in a safe environment where they can learn and grow. Projects should offer opportunities for the intern to demonstrate and develop technical knowledge, problem solving abilities, communication skills and business acumen. Also, the work should allow the interns to understand not only their own roles, but how their work and job function fits into the company overall.

Tim Luzader, Director of Purdue University's Center for Career Opportunities shared a great example illustrating meaningful work from one of his students:

"I had a really great internship experience this past summer. I was an Information Systems Intern along with ~30 others across two locations. Each intern had their own individual project they worked on throughout the summer, but there was also a group intern project. We were split into teams of 6, with 3 of us located in one state and 3 located in another state. We were given the prompt to find a value improvement process (VIP) in the company and estimate the amount of potential savings, showing our approach, ideas, and implementation plan. Towards the end of the summer, we presented our VIP idea and plan in front of IT Directors and Managers who then chose the winning team.

I volunteered to be the project manager for my team which involved a lot of communication and discussion, a task I found difficult when working with multi-site teams. However, it was a rewarding experience for me because I was able to practice my project management skills and learn how to lead meetings and handle conflict. Overall, this was a great project because we had the opportunity to take a vague prompt and make it our own. It also allowed interns to make a difference in the company. We actually implemented our idea and estimated potential savings of $1 million, securing us with a first-place win. Additionally, our project was going to be continued by full-time analysts after we left for the summer. It *is exciting to see that something we investigated for our intern project turned out to be valuable for the company. This internship definitely provided me with some real-world experience and impressive results that I can talk about in future interviews."*

Kim Obergfell - Computer Science Major, Purdue University

Select excellent supervisors and mentors

While meaningful work is important, not having the right supervisor or mentor can make meaningful work painful. A mistake some companies make, is not putting enough thought into who will supervise and/mentor each intern. Often times, a new supervisor is given an intern to get leadership experience. Someone who is a technical expert may not always be the best choice for a supervisor. Also, without proper training, new supervisors may not have the tools to appropriately guide the intern.

Conversely, some seasoned supervisors may not clearly understand the generational differences in having an intern or be too busy in their own jobs to spend the time needed to really develop the intern. Tim Luzader shared one of his student's experiences.

"My first internship with was the definition of a terrible internship experience. I was an eager freshman looking for professional experience so I jumped at the opportunity to work in my hometown (Indianapolis, Indiana) as a Financial Analyst. I quickly learned that the infrastructure of the company was not stable and corporate was not for me. The Vice President of the company quit within the first week of my tenure and I was the only intern in the entire financial division. This led to a generational gap that made it tough for me to make any impact in the company. Since the infrastructure was so fragile my superiors had trouble giving me assignments because they were too overwhelmed to even meet with me. Basically, I saw myself twiddling my thumbs most days and not learned much about financials or budgets for 8 hours a day. "

Jordan Haskins – Accounting and Finance Major, Purdue University

As illustrated in Jordan's recount, it is critical to select the right people to supervise and mentor interns. When the right match is made, incredible things can happen. Take this example from another of Tim Luzader's students:

"It's always great when you get paired with a supervisor who's just as interested in

getting to know you, as much as you're interested in getting to know them and the company. During the summer following my sophomore year, I interned with Turner Construction and was a paired with a great supervisor. With a lot of companies, you don't get to pick your supervisor (so honestly, this is a bit of a gamble), but I was very lucky to be paired with a supervisor who had a really great personality. Every day, she was full of life and energy and we laughed just about every single day. It made coming into work much more enjoyable, and I felt as though, as a result, I performed better and I got more work done. My supervisor was open and honest and always kept communication open for me to be able to ask her questions that really gave me insight into the company. She shared with me her thoughts on diversity in the construction industry and even diversity within Turner. I'll always appreciate the experience I had working with her at Turner that summer. The learning experience was inexplicable."

Danielle Render - Multidisciplinary Engineering Major - Concentration: Engineering Management, Purdue University

Great supervisors and mentors share several common qualities including a willingness to listen and provide on-going guidance.

"Every single person I worked with at my internship was amazing. My supervisor was extremely willing to help and made me feel welcomed from day one. My mentor is one of the reasons I had such an amazing summer. He was always there to answer any questions, helping me get accustomed to things and providing useful insight. I cannot say enough good words about how amazing, helpful and welcoming my supervisor, mentor and the team were. I felt supported throughout my whole project and everyone was extremely friendly and welcoming from the very beginning."

-Anonymous, Chevron Summer Intern 2015

Build an intern community

The last key to making and intern's experience great is to ensure they feel part of a community. A successful intern program should include multiple avenues for interns to network with each other, share experiences and lean on each other for support. Many interns are working in a professional environment for the first time. It can be a scary and sometimes unnerving experience. The intern community provides them a safe environment to bounce off ideas, share information and ask each other questions they may be embarrassed to ask their supervisors. There are many simple and inexpensive ways to help interns connect and engage with each other.

Critical to that sense of community is connecting interns to each other as early as possible. Many companies create a Facebook page, LinkedIn group or other opt in on-line community as soon as the intern accepts. Mediums such as this allow interns to get to know each other in advance, discuss per-assignment jitters and even work out practical things like finding a roommate. Another easy, low cost idea is to host one or more pre-hire webinars that address simple questions about what to expect and that facilitate connecting students virtually. Other companies send a t-shirt or other clothing item the intern can wear proudly on campus prior to starting. This type of swag is like a badge of honor and something to brag about with friends and family.

On the intern's first day, find a way to help them identify each other. Many companies have centralized on-boarding programs to bring all interns together from the start. Another idea is to post a sign with the intern's name and school in their workspace making them identifiable to other interns as well as alumni from their school. At the least, send out an e-mail announcement to the team they are working on introducing each of the new interns.

To bring that community even closer together it's important to have a few group activities scheduled within the first day or week. Have an ice cream social, invite a senior manager to come do a formal welcome, or simply book a room for a brown bag lunch and facilitate a few fun team building activities. I sometimes hear Intern Program Coordinators complain that they have no budget. This should not be a roadblock. Book a conference room and they will come. They usually just need someone to send out the invitation.

In my experience, once some foundational activities have taken place, the intern community begins building their own ways to connect. I have seen some really creative ideas over the years. At one of my former companies I had a group of interns come forward with a proposal to create their own intern council. They asked for a small budget and proposed some great ideas - one of which was coordinating a community outreach project that resulted in collecting over 100 backpacks stuffed with new school supplies for one of our local elementary schools. At another company, I had an intern come to me proposing to coordinate an intern project showcase. This idea resulted in a mini-conference coordinated entirely by the interns. Great ideas come from the intern community so be open to being flexible and allowing for ingenuity throughout the summer.

Conclusion

Reflecting back to my own internship experience, I can clearly say all four of these principals were lacking. There was no reciprocity other than we all laughed a lot together. Grocery shopping and getting people to laugh were not the stimulating work I was hoping for. I don't even remember who my supervisor was and there was no community as I was the only intern in the office. However, my experience did help me shape these principals in developing the various intern programs I have lead over the last 15 year. They are practical, easy to implement and should assist any intern program coordinator in creating a world class internship experience.

References:

NACE (2013). *Professional Standards for University Relations and Recruiting.* Bethlehem, PA: NACE Foundation.

Trending Toward Something New

Tom Borgerding

The job market is changing. The demands to "do more" are increasing. In fact, they are changing faster and demanding more than ever before.

The Bureau of Labor Statistics is reporting that 60% of jobs require a 2+ year college degree and that there will be shortage of nearly 14 million college educated workers by 2020. Those statistics certainly don't help with the pressure of finding the best talent, especially in high demand industries such as accounting, finance, programming, STEM, MIS, and medical fields. With our Baby Boomers getting close to exiting the workforce, there's not just a need to do something new, we are required to come up with ways to bring in new, qualified talent.

Harvard Business Review noted that companies that can successfully manage the end to end journey of applicants will enjoy greater customer satisfaction, less churn, increased revenue and higher levels of employee satisfaction. That sounds great but can be overwhelming regarding how to truly get to that success.

Overlay those statistics and recommendations with student desires for workplace benefits, time off work as personal-time-off or vacation, plus the need of companies to have a larger purpose than to be financially driven - 87% of Millennials believe this. And there's the fact that Millennials touch their smartphone an average of 45 times per day (SDL, Jan 2015) and care more about experiences than material things, the need to diversify and change how career opportunities and company branding needs to change.

Are you ready to do something new? Are you prepared to change to ensure the success of your company and those who work there? Are you prepared to change your trajectory to be where things are going versus where they were?

One statistical trend that is concerning for the recruiting industry is the attention span of Millennials and Generation Z. CMO.com reported that the average length of time a Millennial will focus is 8 seconds while Generation

Z is 5 seconds. This has to be taken into account when we start to think about ensuring truly engaging communication takes place - in person or not. Being on point with your message has to be quick, really quick.

What do we do?

It's time to look at marketing/branding/recruiting holistically and then individually. There is no longer "our message has to be the same across the company." Those days are long gone. Applicants are now looking for the message that "fits them" best...and quickly. There is not much time to engage the applicants...unless they choose to engage you as well. When that happens, they engage and want answers, quickly. What does this look like?

Defining and outline each category below. Each of these will evolve more as new technologies come out but here's where it's trended and trending.

Real conversation

The conversations recruiters are able to have in person need to happen online. Applicants and potential applicants are doing their research in many cases before they ever talk with a recruiter. It's imperative that recruiters are able to find a connection with those they are talking with quickly and individually. What are your interests? What do you like doing? How can I help you achieve your goals? These questions are common in student recruitment.

Intentional engagement

Applicants are turning to the web and the employer's website first (87%) to learn more about a company, what it is like to work there, and if they feel like they are a fit for the organization. The experience on a company careers website should mimic the human interaction while providing more depth and information if the applicant so desires. Applicants will opt to apply or not apply based on those first interactions. Again, try to get there in 5 seconds or less.

A few examples of how to engage students quickly - offer chat and texting with recruiters, use videos to help tell the story, use quizzes or workflows to help applicants determine what may be best for them. Other lighter forms of intentional online engagement include links to social media pages for the company and individuals at the company - not just recruiters, newsletters, announcements, webinars and information sessions.

Intentionally engage applicants. It will take work. They are starting to expect this and will expect this type of engagement more as websites evolve. The technology to engage applicants is available already. Are you willing to invest in intentional engagement with key applicants where they are and not leave it to "change" for your application website to engage the best candidates?

Applicant journey stages

Applicants go through a typical process. That process includes 3 key stages before they truly engage with an employer.

1. Awareness Stage - they need to know you even exist and the basics of why they should care that you do exist. In sales terms, this would be stated "do they even know they have the problem your product addresses."
2. Consideration Stage - they are learning what options exist and which ones they may be interested in pursuing. They are looking at your videos, reviewing Glassdoor, Twitter, Instagram, LinkedIn, and other social media sites to learn more about you.
3. Decision State - they are deciding if your company is the right one for them. Benefits, career paths, learning opportunities, pay, benefits, etc. all come into play.

College Student Applicant's Journey

BUYER STAGES	AWARENESS	CONSIDERATION	DECISION
User Behavior	Has realized and expressed the need for a new degree specific job opportunity	Has defined why and when they want a new degree specific job.	Has defined their strategy, method, and tools to finding a new opportunity.
Research & Info Needs	Research focused on websites and resources with 3rd party information around identifying which careers and jobs of interest/ disinterest.	Committed to researching and understanding all of the available approaches/methods to finding a degree specific job.	Reviewing supporting documentation, data, comparisons, rankings, endorsements to make or recommend a final decision.
Content Types	Websites Career Centers Ads Blog content Expert content/PR Events/Career Fairs Word of Mouth	Websites eGuides & eBooks Live interactions Rankings/Ratings Peers/Parents/Professors Webcast/podcast/video	Employer comparisons Case studies Company employee stories School literature Benefits checklist Live Demo Tour Info Sessions
Key Terms	New job "What is it like to Increase pay be a..." Companies "What would I be good at?"	Engineering jobs Degrees Accounting jobs Location How to apply Rating How to interview	Compare Vs. Pros and Cons versus Best Better Vacation time Benefits Employee feedback Review
Example	What careers am I interested in to study and work? What are those industries like? Do they hire recent grads?	Do I need to get an internship? What do I need to do to get one? Who has internships available?	Which company meets my needs? How do I apply at...?

Personas

Personas are how you define the types of people that are your key applicants and employees. These things can include interests, hobbies, education, degree, gender, ethnicity, personality type, and other things that truly make someone successful at the company. A computer programmer is not the same persona as a financial analyst. A sales rep is not the same persona as a project manager. There may be outliers in each of the personas but use them as a rule of thumb.

Each of these personas are looking for different content that speaks to their interests, desires, and needs. Develop content for each of the Journey Stages that fit each of those personas. This is getting closer to the individual conversation that occurs by a recruiter and a potential applicant. Defining the persona will also help the recruiters customize a conversation with applicants as they get to know each of them. That unique and custom touch point help drive greater engagement. It can also weed out people who don't fit the persona you are looking to hire.

To help you define the personas, look at who is already successful in the business who you want to find people similar. Interview those individuals. Find out their passions, interests, hobbies, pastimes, degrees, etc. Learn from within first. If you have a team of people who are not who you want ideally for the position, use the current team as qualitative information to help to define what you don't want. Either way, learn from experience and within first.

Once you have the personas and applicant journeys defined, then customization to the individual becomes a greater reality. In time, these two will become closer and closer to individual communication as people can define who they are while the content changes to fit those individual personas. When that happens, look out. The companies who use those tools to help move people from "website visitors" to knowing who each person is will win at hiring the candidates that are most engaged with your brand and company. They are also the ones who are most likely to stay at the company the longest.

The Applicant Funnel

The Applicant Funnel is the process that individuals go through to apply at a company. It includes the Applicant Journey and the Personas and various forms of engagement and conversation. To overlay previous section with this one ties the parts together. There are 5 levels in the funnel - Awareness, Interest, Application, Evaluation and Decision.

Level 1 - Awareness

Individuals will become aware of a company in various forms. It can be through a referral by friends and family. It could be through B2B or B2C marketing efforts or publication relations/news stories. Others hear about a company's career opportunities through career fairs, or information sessions, industry websites, job posting sites, search engines, digital advertising such as mobile ads, email, banner ads, and videos, social media, events and tours, magazines, and hundreds of other options.

Which of these awareness channels should be measured, tracked and compared to know where budgets should be allocated? Typically, these are reminders to the target audience that a product, service, company exists and why they should care. This level is where many companies can spend a lot of money but not know what is driving real results for them. We'll talk more about this later.

Level 2 - Interest

People will do one of two things when expressing interest in a company. They will go to friends and families to learn more or they will go online. A rare few will reach out directly to someone at the company to learn more before going to the company website. Expect them to research everything because they will. Online will consist of the company's social media profiles as well as review and feedback websites like Glassdoor.com and Salary.com to get 3rd party - current and past employee - reviews. Millennials and Gen Z expect to be able to find positive and negative reviews about companies which is why it is extremely important for the company to monitor and maintain what they can on these websites.

Additionally, but not exclusively, they will visit the company's website and less to other websites such as careerbuilder.com, glassdoor, indeed.com, and Monster. They may visit the careers page or they may review the products/services offered to decide if they want to learn more about the careers available.

A careers page can then provide specific details for each persona, content for each applicant journey stage and various engagement options including applying (Level 3). That's a simplification of what will be on the careers page but the idea is to ensure that the content available helps each person know the what, why, how, when, who of the company. What that actually looks like on the website will vary from one company to the next. The Interest Level provides the gateway for company specific engagement.

Level 3 - Application

This is the Stage of the Applicant Journey. They are applying. They have already gone through the process of Awareness and Consideration to learn what they need to learn. This likely includes watching videos or reading about career opportunities, team members, corporate values and culture, potentially talking to a recruiter in person or via phone, email, text, or social media.

For those who do not engage this step, digital marketing tools are now available to market to those individuals. It's possible that the person left the website because they were distracted within those 5-8 seconds, weren't interested or wanted to come back later to learn more. Either way, these people are more likely to apply than those who are at the Awareness Level. They have at least made it through the Awareness Stage of the Applicant Journey. Those candidates are more likely to apply than those who have not heard of or are aware of the company as a career opportunity. Dollar for dollar, they are a better investment of marketing and recruiting dollars than someone who is not aware or engaged.

You will notice in the diagram that there is an arrow from the "no conversion" to "retargeting" and back to "your website." Through the use of "cookies," people who have visited your website can have a cookie placed on their device - smart phone/smart device, tablet, computer/PC. If they do not have the cookies turned "off" then those cookies can be used to get your company message in front of the individual after they have left your website. The other hook here is that the cookie would be lost if the individual clears their cookies on their device.

The advertising that can be used to reach these candidates again can include pre-roll videos on sites like YouTube, banner ads on mobile devices, tablet, laptops or PCs. The messages to the individuals can be customized based on which pages were viewed and interests they expressed through their engagement on the websites. "Retargeting" is the act of marketing to someone who has already visited your website by using cookies to identify the device. An example of this is when a student visits your careers page and spends time reviewing the benefits, values and management trainee information pages. When that occurs, the ads can be specific to applying to the management trainee career. There's no reason to not help engage someone with content specific to the Consideration or Decision Stages. Try both if you aren't sure. Help lead them back into the website to apply, connect with a recruiter, ask questions, etc.

Level 4 - Evaluation

The Evaluation Level is when someone has applied to the company and is being reviewed through internal processes. This may include interviews, background checks, and other processes of evaluating if the company feels that individual will be offered a position.

During the evaluation process, messaging to the candidate can continue and be customized to this level of the funnel. Unique messaging based on the positions they are being evaluated for can be used. The candidate is in the Decision Stage as well. They are likely evaluating multiple companies. Continue to engage them to build your employer brand with messages that encourage them to accept if they are extended an offer.

Level 5- Decision

The Decision Level is when the ball is in the court of the candidate to accept or reject your offer. Ongoing messaging from the company through various channels such as email, phone calls, social media and text should continue up to and include this stage. If they say "no" then the message can change. If they say "yes" the messaging can include similar messaging used during the onboarding phase regarding excitement for them to start and looking forward to the impact they will have on the company.

There are stages beyond the Decision Level outlined here. When looking at developing the company brand to people in the Applicant Funnel, these are the 5 Levels. Outline strategies within each so that you do not lose qualified candidates because of a lack of engagement. What does engagement look like? How will you keep moving people through the process or stop the effort to do so if they are not qualified?

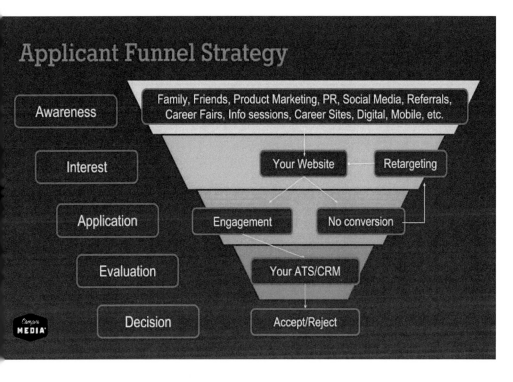

Next steps

What do you do with all of this information? Start simple.

1. Review and define the Personas you are targeting. Don't get so granular that there's only one person who fits the Persona but find the trends within those who want to be part of the company.
2. Use the Persona understanding for engagement from your recruiter team to the candidates as well as on your website.
3. Review your website and add multiple levels of engagement based on the Applicant Journey Stages.
4. Organize your website to have content based on the Applicant Journey Stage. Ensure that all 3 Stages are included on your careers website.
5. Review your messaging in its various forms (website, videos, handouts, presentations, etc.) so that you are quick to the point. Remember you have 5 seconds to engage Gen Z. Ensure you don't lose good candidates because you didn't get to the point.

6. Use various marketing channels including Retargeting to reinforce the messaging, engagement and opportunities at the company. Don't rely only on recruiter conversations with candidates or only technology to drive the final decision. They work best when working together.

Recruiting is changing...fast. Expectations of Millennials and Gen Z has changed as well. Immediacy, responsiveness and access to people and information is expected. Use technology to the advantage of the recruitment team and company. Your candidates are starting to demand individual attention and messaging and will be expecting it more very soon.

Connecting Talent to the Right Experience

Shaunda Zilich

As a Global Employment Brand Leader for a big global company I am **selling experiences** with/at a company. This might be a lifelong experience but many times it is an experience for right now, for this chapter in life. This experience might be a building block for the next or other experiences going on at the same time. My goal or hope is to have it be a win/win. The right experience for the employee and the right experience to further the company. To make this happen there must be 1) truth, 2) I need to sell actual real experiences that 3) connect to a person and their passion.

We can all work on this together to match the right talent with the right experience with these three key elements. First, as companies and marketing professionals we need to paint a picture and tell the story of the true purpose or why a company exists. Second, we all need to journey to discover ours (or another person's) true core passion and purpose. Third, and most important, we need to do a better job of matching the core purpose of each person to the why of a company.

So many times, when we think about the future of careers or even a person's career as it is being discovered we get caught up in the fundamentals of a job. We concentrate on the skills needed or even the culture fit with the company. It is my belief that if we can pair the core purpose of the person and company we will have a great fit (thinking less about a career as ONE thing, ONE skill and more **ONE passion** around a lot of 'careers' or skills).

According to Simon Sinek in "Start with Why" the fundamental difference between the "Apples" of the world and everyone else is that they start with 'why'.

What does that mean? What does that mean to businesses and how can it be translated to careers? Sinek developed what he calls the "Golden Circle". The golden circle has three layers:

1. Why – Core belief of why a business exists.
2. How - How the business fulfills that core belief.

3. What - What the company does to fulfill that core belief.

Sinek states that most companies do their marketing backwards. They start with their 'what' and then move to 'how' they do it. Most of these companies neglect to even mention 'why' they do what they do. There are number of companies that have never thought about the 'why'! This is the same with the way we look at careers. **We look at 'what' a person wants to do and we arm them with skills to complete the 'how' they will do it but we forget to ask the 'why', the core belief they feel is their purpose in life.**

"Why" company's existence

If we think about GE we know (or can discover) 'what' GE does and 'how' GE does it but to Sinek's point we might not know the root cause of 'why' GE exists. If we go down to our core belief GE exists to make a positive impact on the world. Each business we implement and the solutions that we research and drive for are all to make the world a better place. If we base all foundational marketing on this it doesn't matter how many times we pivot, reinvent ourselves, or drive into another industry we will still be core to our 'why' and therefore continue to exist.

GE, and other companies, need to tell more stories of the 'why' to ensure that the branding of the company is true and can (in the end) match the possible candidate's core purpose and passion. This will secure the right talent to the right experience.

Companies can do this in their **own marketing efforts** and with **stories from their employees**.

An example from GE's marketing efforts describes this:

What...
GE makes airplane engines, trains, healthcare equipment.

How...
GE hires top minds in these fields and now (as the new Digital Industrial company) applying data behind the scenes to be sure the airplane or train run on the least amount of fuel, or the healthcare equipment crunches data and

scans to diagnose better and earlier.

Why...

GE is creating ways that airplanes and trains run on the least amount of fuel so that we can save companies money and save the environment. We have healthcare equipment that crunches so much data/years of scans behind the scenes allowing diagnosis and treatment of cancer by data points before the cancer even appears therefore saving lives and our world.

The 'why' mentioned above is what a person, top talent, will connect to emotionally. That is where they will find the right experience for their core passion and gain fulfillment and success.

Example from an employee:

Companies are getting better at letting their employees tell the story. They realize that this provides a transparent point of view for possible candidates and customers to relate. An example of how this can work is below.

What...

A GE Healthcare Technical Writer can simply say she "...is a GE Healthcare Technical Writer". This is the 'what' she does and the 'what' that GE provides as a company.

How...

She can even say, "I write the technical manuals by observing technicians working with the healthcare machines."

Why...

"I am a GE Healthcare Technical Writer. I write the manuals that give doctors and nurses the assurance of knowing they are running the machines correctly and to the best way possible to keep a baby alive in the golden hour after it is born. I write the manuals that give parents the assurance of knowing their child is getting the best healthcare possible."

Telling the story from the 'why' point of view allows a customer or candidate to connect with this company from their inner core purpose, some would say a calling, in their life. This story might even turn career choices to a complete opposite where a story like this encourages someone to work on the 'what' and the 'how' in their career because they connect with the 'why'. It could encourage someone to work on their writing skills and get a degree in technical writing to carry out the 'why', the inner core purpose of their life.

Companies must know why they exist and convey externally why they exist with their own marketing efforts and stories from their employees to attract the right talent.

Passion of the person

What is a person's core belief structure? What is their definition of success? Why are they on this earth? This is something that people do with a 'life coach' or as new year resolutions, however, it is not always what a person does when seeking out their career or next job opportunity.

It is time for us to step back at the way we approach 'finding a career'. Our history has groomed us into thinking of a job as almost a negative thing. Something you must do, and in a lot of cases, something you must suffer through until you retire and get to do what you love. We are in a different environment now. The last two generations have evolved this thinking. Now the three most important things that most the workforce look for in a career is the 1) impact I can make on the world, 2) work/life integration, and 3) growth and development. It almost has nothing to do with skills or 'have to' any longer. It can be something you love to do. We are slowly realizing it doesn't have to be one thing you do all your life to be a 'career'. We put so much stress on this that we don't leave room for those taking part in many different and diverse experiences that ALL share the core passion, the core love, of the person.

Instead of 'finding a career' by what major you take, where you have expertise, and what makes the most money, we need to encourage talent to think about these three things.

1. What are you good at?
2. What do you like to do?
3. What drives you? What is your 'why'? *(the most important question to answer)*

I was recently at a conference where I was so lucky to get to hear Applied Futurist Tom Cheesewright speak. It was interesting to hear his 'future' world. He encouraged us as talent acquisition leaders to stop hiring people for skills that were teachable or repeatable. He made the point that history shows that the future will not need repeatable skills. The future needs skills that cannot be automated. Passion, a person's core belief, a person's 'why', for example, is not repeatable.

In looking at the questions above we can help talent, future candidates, and customers discover what they are good at, what they like to do, and what drives them. There are reasons to walk through each one of these questions. Lining up the answers will allow someone to discover their 'why'. For example, you could be good at robbing banks and even like to do it but chances are it does not line up with what drives you and/or your core belief structure... your 'why' you exist.

I have a friend that would have made a great lawyer. She was amazing at debate and liked the challenge but it did not match up to her core belief structure of why she existed in this world. She didn't always want to have to argue that she was right.

Let's take a moment and look at the possibilities in an example. When I started in college I started as a Vocal Performance major. **I was good at** music, singing, piano, just about any instrument, and I had a flare for acting. I was not afraid to get up in front of people to perform. **I also loved to do it!** I literally felt like I had a 'void' in life and something was missing when I was not preparing or thinking about my next scheduled performance. Looking back, it did follow my core belief. After a few years in my adult life I followed this exercise and have refined it and feel that I exist to positively impact people's lives. My core belief followed what I was good at and enjoyed doing.

Unfortunately, I did not think this way in college. A year into my degree I decided that I was good at math, programming, science, and I should do something with those skills to have a career, to make money. Did I enjoy them? Not really. Did they drive me? No way! I had no idea how they would impact others' lives positively. I finished my degree in Business Management with a lot of programming classes. I then wandered through the next decade wondering why I did what I did everyday didn't make sense to me and I didn't enjoy it.

I truly believe that if I would have **followed the question above I would have realized I could do so many different jobs/experiences with those skills, passions, and beliefs.** My 'career' may have been that I did a variety of things performing music, motivational speaking, counseling with others, etc. In my current role as Employment Brand Leader at GE I can tell you I can answer the three questions above and show why this current role is a great fit for me and for GE.

What if we followed this concept even as parents or trained children to think this way even growing up. Instead of 'waiting or looking forward to see what they become' we realize 'who' they are and 'why' they exist and each step of life help them to find/conquer their purpose. Then we train them to think this way growing up into a job seeker. **Then a career is not something you find or discover rather it is something you always have been and will always be.** There is a much deeper discussion here on the development of the brain however for this purpose we will say that parents/mentors/career counselors can gently guide in thinking about the three questions.

All job seekers (or experience seekers) need to stop, step back, and think of discovering their 'career' in a different way. **Not think about 'what' they will do or 'how' they will do it but 'why' they will do it.** All job seekers need to refer to the three questions above and decide what their future holds. What many experiences their future could hold that all meet the answers to those three questions.

Talent must know why they exist and look to fulfill this existence with everything they do including choosing or making decisions about their career.

Matching passion/why/talent

The last step to connect the right talent to the right experience is to match the passions. To do this - employers need to be sure to showcase the 'why', the impact they make on the world. They need to recruit/attract the right candidates that match this passion. Employees/possible candidates and customers need to be able to think through and know their 'why' and the impact they want to make on the world, the reason for their existence. They need to search out and find the companies that fulfill this passion.

Connecting or matching passion to companies. If this is to be done, then **all need to be transparent and truthful**. As am employment brand leader for a large company I need to tell a truthful story. For GE, we are now this modern, less conservative company but that doesn't mean we don't have hurdles or things that are harder than implementing at a 'start up'. We are not a 'start up' culture yet. We still have growing pains. We are still on the journey. We are still learning from startup companies, from Silicon Valley, from other digital companies that have gone before us, and from mistakes we make. Our employment brand strategy should share the 'what' we are… the 'how' we do it but also the 'why' we do it. Also, that we are not perfect and that if you join our company you might feel some of the bumps in the road but it is worth it… because your passion matches our why and you are helping to complete the journey.

This is a common mantra we use at GE:

At GE, we realize It is not about your career… it is not about your job title… it is about who you are…. It is about the impact you are going to make on the world. You want to go to uncharted waters… do things that haven't been done to make yours and someone else's life better. GE has been and will continue to do that! Join us on this adventure! We are the world's premier digital industrial company.

The action plan:

Companies, recruiters, and employment brand leaders must recruit on passions… on core beliefs. Many times, in the act of recruiting, leaders get more caught up with filling the role or filling a quota instead of making sure they are matching a person's passion with the 'why' of the company.

Candidates must be truthful to who they are. If they have not walked through the three questions mentioned they need discover who they are, why they exist, by doing this exercise. Then they must do their homework and see what companies it matches up against.

Companies and candidates **must match on passions and 'why' each exist.** Both must focus on the concept that it is **fundamentally about connecting companies to the right talent and connecting talent to the right experience.**

Talent Management and Mobility: From the University to the Universe

Peggy Smith

Business has never been more global or more transformative. This interconnected world calls for the ability to identify, attract, hire, place, train and manage an international workforce. Senior leaders have been groomed, through global experience, to operate in a whole-world business context. Younger professionals see global experience as an organic and expected part of their careers: they are open to travel and adventure, and are frequently more mobile than some of their more established colleagues.

As companies worldwide continue to position for growth in both mature and emerging markets, the increased opportunity and expansion strains an already tight labor force. We have known the labor "crash" was coming. Over a decade ago, global demographics on population replacement showed a waning working-age populace in nearly every economy, and coupled with a concurrent out flux of aging workers, demographers and economists could foretell nearly to the year when we would start to feel the pinch in different countries.

If a mobile workforce makes globalization and expansion possible, it makes sense that CEOs consistently cite skills gaps and talent shortages as two of the most critical issues keeping them up at night. These scarcities occur regionally and in several professions. The shortage is often felt most strongly in STEM (science, technology, engineering and math) positions, which can take two to three times as long to fill as other positions. Succession planning is top of mind for most companies, too. With the greying of the workforce, creating a solid leadership pipeline of individuals with robust strategic and business skills is an imperative.

A significant channel to this pipeline is the talent that is nurtured and educated at the university level. ManpowerGroup chairman and CEO Jonas Prising said about corporate success, "To accelerate performance requires that both the public and private sectors work together to prepare the link between business and school." At the same time, universities must meet that challenge by preparing the next generation of leaders for life in this global environment. Today, it can start even earlier. One example is Arizona's partnership with the Harvard initiative, *Pathways to Prosperity*, an effort that creates pathways for children who have interests in IT, bioscience, advanced manufacturing and energy in middle school and high school. As Prising notes, "You can no longer wait until you graduate from secondary schools to decide what you want to do."

Curriculum considerations

Because a global perspective has changed the way businesses operate and grow, the future of undergraduate and graduate business education relies on colleges and universities? considering the tools, programs, equipment and processes currently in use, and what's planned for tomorrow.

Big data is a good example of how a university can design around a business need. The advent of data potential, and the need for experts to collect, parse, and apply those findings has exploded the job market in such areas as HR, marketing, sales, business development, operations, and predictive analytics across all business sectors.

Degrees in international business, or a degree that holds a component of global business, as well as multicultural training and education on multinational perspectives enriches a university's attraction. A focus on corporate social responsibility (CSR) also holds great appeal to young workers. This speaks to a growing desire of young professionals to incorporate transparency and personal values into one's work experience. For the young person heading to a global assignment after university, gaining an understanding of multiple cultures, the environment, social responsibility, infrastructure and community engagement are valuable lessons.

To ready students for globally mobile careers, online business education expands the options for undergraduate and graduate study, making it feasible for someone to attend school or university and work part- or full-time. Better course delivery systems, improved interactivity and discussion, and better multimedia content not only allow students to earn their degrees more flexibly, on their own terms and time, but also opens the opportunity to be educated at a distance. Interestingly, it mirrors the way global and disbursed teams communicate and work together, too – which is another benefit for students, universities and employers.

Feeding the entrepreneurial bent at the university level is also advisable. Younger professionals are now a significant part of the employee community. In 2015, millennials overtook baby boomers in the workplace as the largest generation. In 2017, millennials and GenZ are partnered as employees for the first time. Both generations are observant and selective, and they want to develop their careers in a different manner than those they have seen others commit to. They know that corporations can change someone's career trajectory quickly, so they often position in the workforce in a way that keeps them from being beholden to a corporation. They want autonomy, respect, and collaborative career pathing. Both generations are highly entrepreneurial and innovative, and bring "productive disruption" to the environments where they learn and work.

Since the next big wave of college students and young professionals is GenZ, it's wise to look at their business aspirations to see how to design their educational experience. Nearly 60 percent of GenZ are interested in starting their own businesses. In some regions like the Middle East and Central and Eastern Europe, the figure is close to 75 percent. Given that so many young, talented people could be tempted to start or join a small company with large ambitions, and that more companies are springing up that marry profit with compassion (for example, Tom's Shoes), what do universities need to highlight or improve to capture the attention and consideration of this group? Three initial areas on which to focus are a clear sense of purpose (and meaningful impact on the wider world), scope for personal initiative, and the ability to transition to the workforce with flexibility and independence.

Also in the DNA of young professionals: they think less about their work as a career ladder, and more in terms of a "career lattice." There was a statistic making the rounds a few years ago that set the average time millennials stayed at a job at around 18 months. Younger professionals seem to have found some level of work/life balance that eluded the generations before them. They may end up working more deeply into their later years than their parents *by choice*, but theirs is a work path laced with adventures; with breaks along the way. Understanding this shift can help universities develop coursework that will support this type of career.

Innovation on campus

Employers and educators are learning how to leverage next-gen insight, skills and young professionals' desire for creativity and autonomy. This initiative is helping companies and colleges meet their competition head-on, recruit bright minds and offer a setting where productive disruption is not only welcome, it's encouraged.

Multiple versions of "incubator boot camps" and innovation centers are cropping up where participants can stretch their entrepreneurial muscles and exercise their creativity. A handful of examples include Google's Area 120, Zappos Labs, and Tata Group's design arm, Tata Elxsi. Samsung created a home where great minds and fresh talent can be discovered and nurtured. British Airways even launched *Ungrounded*, its name for innovation lab flights that team up tech talent to solve global air transportation issues. Feeding the entrepreneurial bent at the university level is happening in some major schools, like NYU's Leslie eLabs, accessible across all of the university's schools and colleges, where students can innovate and create. Universities like MIT Sloan, Harvard and Northeastern have entrepreneurial labs, too. These "imaginariums," comparable to start-up cultures, make a unique space for independent originality, collaboration, and experimentation.

Labs and innovation centers are intelligent additions to intelligent industries. On a broad level, by incorporating a start-up model into an existing environment, large companies and institutions can lessen the risk of disruptive technologies from business rivals and start-ups, foster an array of novel ideas for customer-facing products, and give shape to new concepts about purchasing, engaging and connecting online. This shift is changing the nature of R&D, and is a way to keep pace with – or in some cases, outpace – the technology landscape and the industries that are pushed by new technologies.

University-Corporate partnerships

Companies need to train employees, and universities need to increase enrollments. Training and professional development are growing in importance to employees as recruiting tools and benefits. The Georgetown University Center on Education and the Workforce estimates the U.S. spends $772 billion annually on postsecondary education and training, but only about one-third of that amount is directed toward four-year colleges and universities. Some goes to two-year colleges, but the bulk of that investment goes to apprenticeships, industry-based certifications and other programs. Classroom and online training dovetail nicely with corporate partnership programs, presenting a compelling and cost-effective outlet for adult learners for individual courses or full degrees. It's an effective marketing channel for universities, too – the ultimate two-way street that serves the corporation's engagement and education needs and drives registration for the school as well.

University and corporate partnership programs are not a new idea, but they're becoming more prevalent and innovative, with such options as discounted tuition rates that provide a degree at little or no cost to employees, offer university credit for prior learning, make use of corporate partners as adjunct professors, present curriculum that aligns with the corporate mission, have the option of group **corporate classes (to reduce the likelihood of students dropping out or falling behind)** and deliver opportunities for cross-promotion between the organization and the university.

Some schools, like Vincennes University in Indiana, are taking such partnerships a step further, reaching out to students as young as 13 to take part in a Toyota manufacturing education program through an online STEM hub. The college program blends classroom instruction with on-site experience at the Toyota Manufacturing facility in nearby Princeton, Indiana. And though the car company doesn't guarantee jobs after completion of the program, successful graduates are frequently integrated into the company. The company feels that to maintain and grow their talent pipeline, they need to reach high school students earlier and educate them on their programs and opportunities. And the university benefits by earlier and broader enrollment and familiarity with the school.

Competing in the marketplace

By 2018, it is projected that 63% of all jobs in the U.S. economy will require post-secondary education. University-focused individuals are watching the debt that accumulates from an education that may or may not pay off for the investment. They're asking themselves: do I want to start my adult working life with a $350K debt? They've grown up with transparency and comparison shopping, and they make more deliberate and informed choices than their predecessors. That means that universities have more of an imperative to deliver on the value proposition.

In the same way that employers must ratchet up their competitive game with other companies vying for the same talent, so must universities increase their appeal. CEOs of public and private corporations are alerted by shifts in business and workforce trends that are affecting their current strategy, or that will impact their futures. Universities and colleges must do the same. So, for example, when we learned some years ago that by 2018, three million STEM workers would be needed, the universities that jumped on that information, recruited more STEM-directed students, increased their capabilities and reputations for teaching these functions will be frontrunners in that field.

Public and private universities, to a certain extent, can leverage their brands and names – but a more discerning influx of students is looking beyond their college years to the workforce. Universities that are better at connecting students with employers increase their appeal.

Trends and opportunities

Some of the trends that corporate CEOs are addressing, and that universities and colleges can evaluate for their importance to recruiting students include:

- **An awareness that transparency is woven into younger generations.** They are the ultimate comparison shopper: they are unafraid of challenging everything to get to a better financial or logistical outcome; they seek and force transparency in every aspect of their lives.
- **More integration of diversity and inclusion.** Demonstrate the objective of making talent development a priority, and of opening opportunities across the organization.
- **Increased parity, and a narrowed gender gap.** Mercer, in its *"When Women Thrive"* research, notes that female representation declines as career level rises. Globally, women make up 33% of managers, 26% of senior managers, and only 20% of executives. Mercer points out that by 2025, women will still represent only 40% of the workforce at and above the professional level, and says, "Organizations need to focus on systemic, supporting practices to build the female talent pipeline that will sustain gender equality in the

long term."

- **Alternative employment options, like the gig economy.** A 2016 McKinsey Global Institute study revealed that the number of independent workers had been undercounted, and makes up 20-30 percent of the labor force in both the U.S. and the EU-15. Workers with specialized skills and in-demand experience win in the gig economy; they can create a career that incorporates flexibility, autonomy, and meaning. Younger generations are seeing this, too: in a Universum Global study, fifteen percent of the GenZ individuals surveyed said they would be willing to forgo college in favor of alternative schooling, such as apprenticeships, and 60 percent were interested in learning how companies can educate people who haven't attended conventional universities.

- **Changes in how companies source employees.** Enabled by technology and social media, companies are sourcing talent differently than they did even few short years ago; running multiple searches across multiple sources; working more efficiently with resume databases; developing strong recruitment and sourcing strategies; and maintaining awareness of what types of jobs, locations, benefits and perks are appealing to different generations in the workforce. For universities, understanding the way companies in different industries are sourcing talent can help guide students toward employment while earning or after earning their degree.

Companies that want to grow, that wish to build teams or organizations capable of innovating, must be aware of the tools, policies, training and recruiting strategies required to engage and sustain a range of workers and perspectives in the workforce. The same is true for colleges and universities. It's possible to create a natural flow of well-prepared future global business leaders that emerge from the university and are directed to the universe of companies hungry for skilled job candidates; engaged and gifted professionals who can support expansion and strategic initiatives, and add constancy and succession possibilities to the talent pipeline.

References:

Carnevale, Anthony P.; Smith, Nicole; Strohl, Jeff. (2010) *Projections of Jobs and Education Requirements Through 2018*: Georgetown University Center on Education and the Workforce.

Deloitte (2015) *Building Competitive Advantage:* Bersin by Deloitte

Glassdoor.com (2016) *Benefits Reviews*

KPMG (2016) *2016 Global CEO Outlook*

Manpower Group (2016) Emerging Global Motivators & Job Search Preferences:

Mercer (2015) *When Women Thrive*

McKinsey Global Institute (2016) Independent Work: Choice, Necessity and the Gig Economy

Universum Global (2016) *Gen Z in the Workplace Report*

From Campus to Business Results

Ripp Kardon

Part 1 - Confirmation bias

"You've got to think about big things while you're doing small things, so that all the small things go in the right direction". Alvin Toffler

Just by holding this book in your hand we know you are passionate and enthusiastic about campus and university recruiting. Like me, you love being on campus with the students and finding talented students that inspire and energize you and your organization.

Passion and enthusiasm are the fuel for success in almost all parts of life and work, without them everything from relationships to careers will fail.

Take a step back from those feelings that inspire and drive you.

Detach yourself from the new initiative you are working so hard on.

Block out those tactical and possibly fun ideas you have for your campus recruiting efforts in the coming months.

Ask yourself a few key questions

1. How aligned and connected is your campus/university recruiting program to your organization's goals and long term strategy?
2. Is your Campus Recruiting strategy helping your company close essential skills gaps?
3. If someone asked your client what his/her talent strategy goals were and then asked you the same question, do you feel confident you would have the same answer?

Campus Recruiting and Talent Acquisition as a whole make the greatest impact and are true judicious partners when aligned with the business strategy.

If talent is the most valuable commodity an organization can have, why would you supply anything short of the most precise and symbiotic talent?

Feeling confident that you are aligned to your company's goals is easy. We rationalize and justify our efforts and hard work by telling ourselves and others that "yes, we are in lockstep with that c-level executive"

Don't allow yourself to fall victim to confirmation bias.

Take a deep and critical look at your day to day and your long-term strategy. Do they support where your organization is trying to go in next 1, 3 or 10 years?

Look around, make sure you are not on an island.

Part 2 - Models for winning

"You can have the best strategy and the best building in the world, but if you don't have the hearts and minds of the people who work with you, none of it comes to life."
Renee West, Blackrock

STEM campus recruiting is generally regarded to be the most competitive industry to recruit for, but not far behind is the hyper competitive and talent voracious world of financial services.

Blackrock currently sits as the world's largest asset manager with 5.1 trillion in assets and 12000 employees worldwide. Started in only 1988, the firm's talent and campus strategy are major reasons why the company has experienced such prodigious success in 30 years. Blackrock's rise to a global influencer status came in 2008 when it was selected by the US Government to support the turnaround of the Great Recession. It continues to be ranked as one of the world's most admired and desirable employers.

The company's strength comes in its progressive approach to talent acquisition and campus recruiting. It is a belief that stems from the executives down.

Although the HCC (Blackrock's Human Capital Committee) leaves talent tracking and workforce planning to the leaders of the various businesses, it is actively engaged in employer branding. Recognizing that the firm needed to tailor its appeal to a new breed of college and business school graduates, members of the HCC worked with the marketing team to devise a campus recruiting campaign that addresses two of the highest priorities among young people: career mobility and social responsibility.

In a rapidly changing global economy where speed and agility define success, they have built a culture of talent development that starts on campus.

Recognizing the vital need to attract the best students on campus their "global graduate recruitment program is built on strong relationships with local universities and business schools."

Doing this drives their talent pipeline and produces a workforce that is "diverse in thought, race and gender". With a diverse employee population, they are able to reflect/resemble and deliver on the needs of their global book of clients.

General Electric

One of the greatest efforts of a company to reinvent and recalibrate its talent strategy to its business needs is General Electric.

In one of the most groundbreaking and aggressive efforts to attract talent and show the company's changing talent strategy, they began a national TV ad campaign called "Owen". The creative and informative ads featured a recently hired soon to be college graduate explaining to his friends that he was hired as a developer to write code for the machines that GE builds for trains, planes and electric infrastructure.

This ad campaign was part of the overall talent strategy set by GE CEO Jeff Immelt. In 2010 Jeff and GE "had to decide how to respond to the digitization of the industrial sector". GE already dominated the industrial sector and had for 50+ years. In the face of a growing digital world they had to align their talent strategy to close the talent gap and position themselves for a talent transformation.

"So, what you're going to do is you're going to blend (new technology focused hires) with the GE team, and then we're going to recruit differently. When we go to college campuses, we're

going to look for different skills. We're going to put them in different training programs. It's a combination of we've got to bring our culture along, but that's not enough. We've got to bring thousands of people in from the outside. That's the only way we're going to get there fast enough." Jeff Immelt

Part 3 - Weaving the campus recruiting fiber

"Performance more often comes down to a cultural challenge, rather than simply a technical one." Lara Hogan, Etsy

In building strong programs at Blackrock and GE, a campus recruiting fiber was woven into the fabric of their company cultures.

Building a campus program that is part of an organization's culture is the foremost indication of its success. Employees from the CEO to the most junior of associates should understand and support the campus recruiting efforts and how it enables the organization.

New and developing campus recruiting programs must embrace the reality that they are not just recruiting talent, but also helping to shape a company's culture one hire at a time and one manager at a time.

Partnering with leaders and managers to reshape their perspectives on college talent and provide positive experiences in working with campus recruiting is often your greatest opportunity.

In building or revamping an early career programs, it is vital that a deep analysis of a company's talent needs is executed and a methodical effort is made to understand and keep up with those needs.

When leaders see campus talent directly contributing to performance there is a value created and an appetite for college talent takes root.

Getting to this point can take an enormous investment of time, finances and hours. Any new or developing campus program must make the value proposition that hiring college talent will pay dividends. The average cost per hire for campus and experienced hires is surprisingly similar.

Campus Hire: $3,582 Vs. Experienced Hire: $4,129

Developing early career professionals is not for those seeking a quick return on investment. The people hours and cost of recruiting, hiring, training and developing entry level talent is not for all organizations. The quickest contributions to organizational growth tend to come from experienced hires that come closer to ready right out of the offer letter box.

Smaller firms that need a quick financial return likely can't justify Campus Recruiting. For organizations willing to commit to the long game, develop the culture and hire the right talent, the results can transformative.

Recent college graduates bring a plethora of diversity types, energy and enthusiasm, newer skills, ways of thinking, innovation and the desire to grow and be developed. Financially they can bring tremendous returns in the ways of product, process and sales development.

Part 4 - Stay the course

"Discipline is the soul of a successful army. It makes small numbers formidable; procures success to the weak, and esteem to all." George Washington

Success does not come from a moment of inspiration, no matter how great the quote or YouTube video. Inspiration is only the spark. Success comes from a daily commitment to staying consistent and unwavering in the face of doubt and being regimented in your practices.

The examples of Blackrock and GE campus recruiting operations come from understanding the direction and needs of their business and setting a strategic talent vision.

How does Campus Recruiting stray from their path and go off their game plan? What are the key elements that need to be consistent?

Set your competencies and skill set

What are the hard and or soft skills the company must have? Conduct a deep dive to identify what the organization or particular department must have to be successful. Once aligned and committed to with the business do not waver. The long-term return will far outweigh any short-term gain that could come from diverting from the skills and competencies.

Pick your schools (and stick with them!)

Identify the schools that provide the talent you need, can afford and make sense geographically. Commit to your "core schools" for a minimum of 12 months and evaluate after. Like any relationship, the more you invest with your partner and the more you commit to them, the more they can give to you. Everyone feels their alma mater should be a core school. Ask a business leader what schools you should be recruiting and you are very likely to receive an opinion impacted by a litany of biases.

Use data and analytics to build the business case of why each core school is vital to your long-term talent game plan.

On campus go high, deep and wide.

Go high by connecting and building your brand with the deans and senior leaders on campus that can advocate and support your efforts.

Go deep by building relationships with the vital support staffs that enable your success.

Go wide by reaching across campus (if possible) touching all of the programs and schools on campus that can be a pipeline of talent.

Don't just take.

Be a true partner to your schools and find ways to give back. If you have fiscal restrictions, your organization's time, knowledge or resources can be just as valuable in helping your school prepare their students for graduation.

Interviews designed to identify competencies and skills

Build a robust, challenging and interesting interview process that takes input from all parts of your organization. There are thousands of interview processes out there and even more opinions on which are the best. The best process is the one identifies the best hires with the competencies, skills and experience that will solve your talent needs. Let the process tell your story, show your culture and maybe just maybe... let the students have a little fun.

Part 5 - Prove it

"If we have data, let's look at data. If all we have are opinions, let's go with mine."
Jim Barksdale

We live in a word that is quality becoming reliant and driven by data. Everything from healthcare to your internet experience is driven by data and analytics.

Sales or business development function uses a CRM tool religiously to drive revenue.

Internal IT teams are consistently looking for faster more efficient ways to support and monitor their end users.

Marketing teams are obsessed with collecting, tracking and analyzing data from their online efforts.

Human Capital/ Human Resources, Talent Acquisition and Campus Recruiting are some of the last business functions to embrace and leverage this paradigm shift.

Why?

- Do we not have the tools?
- Do we resist the thought that people can become defined by a statistic?
- Do we want to keep the "human element" as the key part of our jobs?

As a function, we need to embrace measurement, data and analytics as a way to lead our organizations forward. Looking at the most successful and progressive organizations over the last 10 years shows that using data to help make talent strategy decisions is a proven practice. Google is the most popular and successful example. Its (data driven HR) approach has resulted in Google producing amazing workforce productivity results that few can match (on average, each employee generates nearly $1 million in revenue and $200,000 in profit each year.

Campus Recruiting Starting Point

Establish a process or tool that collects data from all Campus Recruiting events. Understand how many candidates you are touching per event. From the career fair to on campus interviews, be able to explain where these students come from and if they meet the needs set forth in your organization's strategy.

Track and Collect Data Throughout Process

- Campus interviews
- Final interviews
- Offers
- Acceptances
- Diversity
- Major

These are just a handful of the data points that are tracked in an impactful campus program. All parts of the process should be collected to help support your decisions. Evaluate this data and use it to select your "core schools" and evaluate your schools every 12 to 18 months.

You may find that just because you have a great brand and lot of traffic at a university that is not translating into offers or successful hires.

Post Hire Data

Work with your internal HR Partners and business leaders to track your campus hires once they are in the organization. The data collection should not stop at the offer stage.

- What campus hires are the strongest performers?
- What "core schools" are provide the longest employee tenure?
- What majors are providing the greatest ROI?

Understand if Campus is truly delivering business results by measuring campus hires vs. other forms of hires.

- Performance
- Objectives / Goals
- Productivity
- Retention
- Employee engagement

This information is vital to strengthening campus recruiting position within an organization or to recalibrate and adjust strategy when needed.

From Campus to Winning the War

Campus recruiting should not be a "nice to have" or a "feel good" program owned by HR. It is not a support program to help employee family members build their resumes with internships. It is not inexpensive labor for the summer or a few weeks.

Successful organizations use it as a competitive advantage that endow them to win the war for talent and ultimately drive business results.

Commit to and deliver this these tenets to your organization and Campus Recruiting will become an essential partner to the business.

Additional Resources:

https://en.wikipedia.org/wiki/BlackRock

http://www.economist.com/news/leaders/21591174-25-years-blackrock-has-become-worlds-biggest-investor-its-dominance-problem

https://hbr.org/2014/01/building-a-game-changing-talent-strategy

https://hbr.org/2014/01/building-a-game-changing-talent-strategy

https://www.msn.com/en-us/money/video/larry-fink-how-blackrock-attracts-top-talent/vi-AAhkDmc

http://www.mckinsey.com/business-functions/organization/our-insights/ges-jeff-immelt-on-digitizing-in-the-industrial-space

http://www.mckinsey.com/Videos/video?vid=4546787234001&plyrid=2399 849255001

https://www.naceweb.org/uploadedfiles/content/static-assets/downloads/executive-summary/2014-recruiting-benchmarks-survey-executive-summary.pdf

https://www.shrm.org/about-shrm/press-room/press-releases/pages/human-capital-benchmarking-report.aspx

https://www.eremedia.com/ere/how-google-became-the-3-most-valuable-firm-by-using-people-analytics-to-reinvent-hr/

The Tech Frontier

Bryan Quick

There is no doubt that advancements in technology are having a significant impact on how organizations engage and hire top talent. It is also safe to say that the recruiting organizations that embrace tech tools along with this new environment will prevail setting their organization apart in a sea of competition. Employers are racing to innovate this space and implement the next new technology with the hope to win the war for talent. In this essay, we will explore a few guiding principles to the increasing role that technology is having and some effective methods to consider in order to build a successful strategy. To do this, we will break down the discussion of technology into a few prevailing concepts. These concepts have been agreed on by talent acquisition professionals across multiple industries to be imperative to consider during strategic planning.

An organization's technology strategy should be tailored to the needs of the business.

With the introduction of new technologies emerging more frequently and traditional solutions to recruitment consistently evolving, making the right decision on the tools to utilize becomes more difficult. Picking the right recruitment technologies can make an immediate and dramatic impact on an organization's talent acquisition strategy. The key is to avoid getting overwhelmed. Ensure that the strategy supports the business needs, how success will be measured, and above all the candidate experience. Even educated guesses could be wrong, but organizations can do well by leveraging data-driven performance metrics important to their group and ensure that these are discussed in initial talks with any vender of a new technology before jumping into the waters of a new tool.

Recruiting organizations need to engineer mobile-friendly engagement.

In today's world, mobile is king. Candidates want employers to meet them on their turf…on their smart phones and devices. Almost 50 percent of job applicants globally now search and apply for jobs using a mobile device. At the very least, employer career pages should be optimized for the mobile experience. This allows the employer to reach passive candidates much more easily, but if done well, it can provide a great impression of the brand. Beyond the career page, employers should think about improving other aspects of the mobile user experience. This would include creating a mobile-friendly application process and improving your load times as much as possible. These two factors will lose potential candidates if they aren't fast and easy to use.

By focusing on building a robust mobile strategy, whether by optimizing company content or enabling video interviews with mobile friendly applications, employers can enhance their brand by creating an easy and accessible candidate experience. It is also an effective way for recruiters to extend their talent pool. Passive candidates are often disengaged because the mobile capabilities of the organization lack the outreach necessary to target them successfully.

High tech meets high touch with new advents in CRM technology

About 70% of talent acquisition groups say that they currently use some form of Applicant Tracking System (ATS). At its core, the ATS functions to document applicant records, maintain a history of candidate recruitment activity as well as the majority of hiring activity that is not captured by the human resource information system (HRIS). They tend to be the only systems where recruiting related information on a candidate can be found. An ATS is also used in many cases out of necessity to comply with laws like OFCCP or EEOC. Although this can be an important system for recruiters, the information in an ATS can become outdated very quickly which can limit the effectiveness of the tool. Most recruiters end up using the ATS as a "just in time" tool only and not as a way to engage candidates.

When companies come across top talent with the kind of knowledge, skills and abilities that might be a good fit for future positions or align with a respective employer's recurring recruiting needs, ATSs do a poor job of enabling the recruiters to actually manage, nurture and engage with any candidate in the system who might be right, just not "right now". It is for this reason alone that recruiting organizations will and should continue to move towards the use of a customer (candidate) relationship management tool (CRM). As CRMs, which have traditionally made a home in sales and marketing organizations, become more prolific in talent acquisition, a new role in recruiting has emerged that has transformed traditional recruiters and sourcing groups into marketers. Their job now is to run targeted job campaigns and continue to engage passive candidates that may have already established a relationship with the company. The CRM allows those professionals to utilize information that is captured through job campaigns, online events, and even on campus to proactively engage each contact in the system.

Organizations should focus on engagement as the new form of sourcing

Many recruiters and talent acquisition organizations say that most of their time is spent on sourcing. Yet, at the same time, while they spend more time than ever on sourcing, it has become more difficult than ever to engage the right people. With job boards, candidate aggregators and social media platforms, it may be easier to find the talent but now the challenge is how to keep them engaged. Candidate engagement has become much more important in recruiting than ever before.

When thinking about making candidate engagement more efficient and effective, there are two talent technology keys every employer should consider. First, recruiting organizations need time to engage. It is the nightmare of every recruiter: finding the time to post the job, schedule interviews, make offers and somewhere, in that whirlwind of activities, try to keep the candidate informed, engaged and excited about the opportunity. It's easy to understand how a candidate can get lost in the shuffle. By finding ways to reduce all of that logistical work of sourcing that most recruiters find themselves tasked with, they are able to spend more time engaging top talent and building the kind of relationships needed to transform a passive seeker into an active candidate.

Companies must make every effort to communicate early and often with candidates. This will reduce the risk of losing top talent to more agile companies by ensuring a timely and collaborative candidate communication strategy in place. Set applicant response time goals, such as 24-hours for new applications, in order to hold each team member responsible and utilize a CRM tool to automate the messaging. Incorporate more touch points into the candidate interview lifecycle by automatically sending candidates and interviewers' reminders before and after their scheduled interviews.

Secondly, organizations need to embrace and find ways to optimize the process of sourcing candidates by utilizing tech tools like the CRM discussed earlier along with other digital or virtual platforms. Most CRMs, for example, allow the organization to create job marketing campaigns that are tied to specific jobs and control communication after the candidate applies to a job with branded messaging that is tailored to each candidate. Furthermore, many CRM tools can integrate with an ATS allowing for a seamless candidate experience. By incorporating tools that utilize the branded messaging and media to tell the story of the organization, the right candidates get a better picture of the company they are considering and in turn are more likely to accept their offer to join that organization.

Some employers are also transitioning traditional corporate information sessions into virtual sessions. By utilizing tools like Google Hangouts, ViewPoint, WebEx and others, recruiting organizations now have the ability to connect with more candidates outside of the on-campus recruiting events.

Go social and get mobile

Even though social recruiting isn't new, or even a new trend, there are a few social media tactics that will continue to become more popular. Perhaps the most crucial way to use social media in recruiting is to use it as a referral source. Over 30% of companies saw an increase in their referral candidates once engaged in social recruiting, and referral candidates are often the ones who stick around longer and perform better in their positions.

However, the big trick with social media is to not get too carried away, and to remember to have a relationship with potential candidates. Social media doesn't mean that you don't have to talk to candidates, or that you should only tweet jobs, or that social media recruiting is free because the platforms are free to use. Social recruiting has its own set of best practices, much like the recruiting process itself.

Mobile recruiting has also seen a significant expansion in the past 5 years. Almost 50% of job seekers search and apply for jobs using a mobile device. At the very least, employer career pages should be optimized for the mobile experience. This allows the employer to reach passive candidates much more easily, but if done well, it can also provide a great impression of the brand. Sixty-one percent of people said they have a better view of the brand based on the mobile experience. Beyond the career page, employers should think about improving other aspects of the mobile user experience. This would include creating a mobile-friendly application process and improving your load times as much as possible. These two factors will lose potential candidates if they aren't fast and easy to use.

Recruiters can also use mobile recruiting apps to capture candidate information and resumes at career fairs, diversity conferences or classroom presentations. They can eliminate reviewing paper resumes, and evaluate candidate information at any point on a phone or tablet without logging long hours in front of a computer or sifting through piles of paper.

Virtual interviews are the new normal

Businesses today are becoming increasingly global and interconnected in a new world economy that crosses geographies and cultures. While the global economy has affected large employers in the past, smaller companies are starting to emerge on to the scene with hiring objectives that span beyond their headquarters. These companies will also have to cope with the challenges of multiple recruiting teams that hire for many functional areas in different countries. It is always difficult and often frustrating for recruiters to coordinate ever changing interview schedules for both the candidate and the hiring managers especially in a remote environment. This has led to recruiting organizations focusing on technologies that allow more flexibility in the interview process.

Video interviewing technologies are increasingly becoming an integral part of the recruiter toolkit. Some companies embrace the video interview by using low or no cost services such as Skype or Google Hangouts as opportunities to meet and greet candidates live over the web. More robust video interviewing software, like Avature or HireVue which are systems that integrate nicely with ATSs and CRMs, contain video interviewing features or functionalities to create a more candidate friendly, integrated and low cost approach to the initial screening process and beyond. These tools allow candidates to manage their own interview by selecting interview times that work for them on their own time. The candidate can record their responses via video and it is uploaded and sent directly to the hiring team for a decision. Candidates also have the flexibility to reschedule these interviews more easily without disrupting the recruiting organization.

No doubt, this shift in how a company performs an interview will continue to affect the overall candidate experience. It is important for employers to consider this impact on the candidate and ensure that appropriate communication is in place to assist them in making this adjustment. Otherwise, there is a strong risk the process will be viewed negatively as a cost-cutting measure alone.

Use technology to leverage the right data and metrics

With hiring managers and business leaders increasingly looking for more understanding and measurable results throughout their business, it's imperative for recruiters to provide meaningful metrics and actionable insight into the talent function's overall process and results. More refined hiring metrics mean getting a better look at where the issues are, which hiring managers or recruiters are the most effective, and what's really working in recruiting – and what's not.

By placing focus on gathering the right data, hiring departments will be able to better benchmark their hiring results and learn what really constitutes hiring success. Traditionally, recruiters have been evaluated almost exclusively on KPIs (key performance indicators) like time to fill or cost per hire. Unfortunately, this method focuses too much on the sheer number of hires that are brought in through the process ignoring important controls regarding quality of hire, candidate engagement or the recruiter's overall impact on organizational recruiting or staff retention. In the future, you can expect recruitment organizations to start seeing a shift from transactional to strategic performance metrics. The overall performance will be measured by the real value and work that they bring to the business.

Where technology comes in is by leveraging data and performance metrics to measure the impact of certain campus and diversity conferences. Tools like a CRM can help track the number of hires, engagement points with each candidate and overall expenses per recruitment marketing effort, like career fairs, so you can report out the exact return on investment.

Concluding thoughts

Recruitment technology truly is the new frontier in engaging the talent of tomorrow and reporting the successful outcomes of that engagement. Every organization is different in the approach they may take to embrace this new, high tech world. Although many of the concepts mentioned here are applicable to any industry, it is important to remember that some tools and strategies work better than others depending on the size and complexity of the organization. One thing remains true. Technology should exist as a bridge to a better overall experience for the candidate and we hope the concepts discussed in this segment provide helpful context to this exciting time in the field of talent acquisition.

References:

Ali, M. (2015). Tech Trends of 2015. Retrieved from SHRM Article http://www.shrm.org/hrdisciplines/staffingmanagement/articles/pages/recruiting-tech-trends-2015.aspx

Futurestep (2014). Futurestep predicts top five talent acquisition trends for 2015. Retrieved from: http://www.futurestep.com/news/futurestep-predicts-top-five-talent-acquisition-trends-2015/

Leveraging Social Media

Christopher Carlson

Social media can be a powerful, and sometimes intimidating, tool for an organization's recruiting strategy. At the heart of the social media value proposition is the premise that it makes a much-needed personal connection with the candidate, eliminating, or at least minimizing, the impersonality of online applications. The vast majority of companies leverage applicant tracking systems, and most colleges have an online system for collecting resumes and posting positions. Nothing is less personal. Students may receive a generic email thanking them for applying or a polite, and often impersonal, rejection notification, but that's it. The transactional nature of applying does nothing to brand your organization or encourage future applications from that candidate. Personal connections and tailored marketing have now become an integral part of employer branding, and that is where leveraging social media can make a noticeable difference. If a company is competing for talent, this personalization becomes that much more important in enticing the candidate to apply, remain engaged, and ultimately accept an offer. Sustaining that connection is a challenge and it is critical to address that challenge effectively.

Key components

From my perspective, there are two critical components of building a social recruiting strategy. The first is really about content, messaging and branding. To start down this path, I recommend looking at different components of traditional campus recruiting and how they translate into a virtual world. The content that is developed for the virtual world needs to be both engaging and compelling so that individuals will return time and time again. That component takes some time to develop as you need to think about (1) how you deliver your message across all the outlets, (2) how you highlight your employee value proposition and (3) how you enhance the candidate's experience. You can't just tweet: "We have jobs!" or "Hey you! Here is a job for you". People will get bored with that very quickly. You will need to translate the key messaging from your traditional campus information session into virtual messaging and balance that messaging with your technical and functional expertise that you share in classroom presentations or case

competitions. You also have to think about how to reach as many candidates as possible and then drive those connections into your pipeline. There are a number of companies out there that do a tremendous job with this component and have been doing so for a while, so it is important to think about how to set your company apart.

The second component is one that many old-school recruiters may appreciate – "direct sourcing". In the days before the internet, it was essential for a recruiter to know how to start with a list of five names and turn those into a pipeline. Today, great talent exists across many universities and there are traditional students and non-traditional students. The rise of tools like Handshake that opens up opportunities to all students across a multitude of campuses shows that the pool of candidates is expanding beyond just the traditional core school model. The social media approach must also allow for these direct interactions that are scalable and sustainable, so as to reach the top talent regardless of campus.

Reaching a diverse audience

One of the most difficult aspects of creating a social media presence is building an audience. A great way to begin reaching potential candidates is to leverage your current employees for building your new network. In many cases, alumni, recent graduates, and your current interns provide the best way to establish rapport quickly.

Another approach is to identify key individuals across ERGs or other employee groups to serve as social media ambassadors. Provide them with tips and tools for sharing content that shows what it is like to work at the company and have a list of recommended hashtags and identifiers so that they can contribute to your collective presence online. When hosting webinars, you may want to consider engaging recent graduates to lead the conversations and encourage them to provide their perspectives on working at the company.

Some key points to consider in developing your strategy include the following:

- *Use multiple channels to share your message.* Different platforms have different styles, reach different audiences, and are used for different reasons. Diversify your outreach to use a variety of platforms that work with best for your particular organizational and/or departmental goals.
- *Make your content diverse and inclusive.* Work closely with your marketing team to ensure your images are not only high-quality, but that the content shows the diversity of your workforce and your space. Encourage staff to use gender appropriate terminology, interchanging "he" and "she" and "they" in examples and pictures. Candidates want to see that your space and your organization will be a good fit, so make sure your images reflect your mission and your company culture.
- *Make it standard.* It is essential that your voice and your message are standardized and consistent, no matter what staff or team member is posting. Your audience should be able to recognize your organization's content and message regardless of what platform they are viewing it on.

Personal versus private

Remember one of the primary reasons students are on social media is to interact with their social networks, i.e., their friends. There is an old adage "there is a time and place for everything and it is called college". Although social content exists for all time, it is important to remember that students do not always want employers to view or access their posts.

Social media approaches need to remain more of a push rather than a pull. Just as a company representative would not recruit at a fraternity or sorority party, recruiters must remember that not all social media outlets are sources for engagement. Identifying ways to reach students on platforms that allow for sharing of your information, without sharing theirs, is a great place to start. Some platforms allow this more easily, such as Instagram and Twitter, whereas other platforms lean more toward personal student information, such as Facebook and Snapchat. Starting with passive participation platforms can be an easier way to begin your strategy, streamline your message, and clarify your voice, before branching out into higher touch apps.

Likewise, leveraging your employees in your approach requires a conversation about privacy. Many of your employees, including talent acquisition staff, may not have a marketing background or an interest in social media. Help your colleagues become more familiar with the platforms you've chosen, so they understand the value as well as the nuances of each app. Develop tips for social media engagement and best practices for staff who are marketing opportunities and events. Encourage staff to share real-life pictures and posts to better present a realistic view of your company culture. Students will expect what they have come to perceive, so be honest with your representation and what they can anticipate at your organization.

Final thoughts

In whatever ways you execute your social media recruitment, it is critical that you are (1) personalizing your value proposition through messaging, pictures, and posts; (2) enhancing candidate engagement (3) reaching diverse audiences, and (4) building a long-term talent community. The channels you choose will depend on your company's demand and your resources. As noted, it is more important than ever to brand your company as an employer of choice. Reaching the talent your company needs may very well extend beyond your list of "core schools" or require you to compete with better brands that hire large numbers of college students. It is essential that you can develop an approach to social media that will position your company at the forefront of the audience you are trying to reach. It is not a one size fits all approach but instead a customized strategy that will require you to engage key stakeholders across your organization including marketing, communications, employee groups and employees. Remembering that once you work to establish a presence on social media, it will be there for all to see, so make sure you have a clearly defined approach with key messages for the audience you wish to attract.

Any views and opinions expressed in this essay are attributable to me and do not necessarily represent the opinions of the Tennessee Valley Authority or the U.S. government.

References:

Agrawal, S. (2014) "How Companies Can Attract the Best College Talent", March 17, 2014, Harvard Business Report.

Mobile Recruiting: Will It Drive a Revolution in How Employers Evaluate Career Services, Job Boards, and Other Sources of Hire?

Steven Rothberg

One of the benefits of having more than two decades of experience in the worlds of college recruiting and employment marketing is that you're better able to recognize patterns and even predict outcomes. The buzz that started years ago and continues today about whether and how employers should engage with candidates using mobile devices such as smartphones and tablets is startlingly similar to the conversations being held in the mid-1990's when employers were struggling to come to grips with this thing called the Internet.

For those too young to remember and those too old to care to remember, only 20 years ago the vast majority of college students and recent graduates applied to the vast majority of jobs pretty much the same way they did in the 1950's: by getting a printed copy of their resume into the hands of a recruiter. The popularization of the fax machine in the 1980's sped up the process of getting that resume from a candidate in one location to a recruiter in another, but the end result was the same: the recruiter had a printed copy in her hands of the candidate's resume and placed it for review along with other resumes collected at career fairs, on-campus recruiting, and via what we now call snail mail.

Suddenly, the world changed. The Internet as we know it today came into being in 1994 when Netscape's browser went mainstream and the masses were, for the first time, able to access the Internet through this revolutionary interface called the World Wide Web. The vast majority of Fortune 500 companies did not have websites, few of those had career sections on their sites, and none of those career sites made it easy for candidates to search for and apply to jobs. Over the next decade, employers large and small invested vast sums of money into their career sites, applicant tracking systems (ATS) were born and took control of the recruiting process for many of these organizations, resumes flowed in at a rate never seen before, but neither candidates nor employers were any better off.

Tracking software has existing for 20+ years

The technology has existed since the mid-1990's to track a consumer from their viewing of an advertisement on a third-party website to the advertiser's website to their registration to their purchase of a product or service. College Recruiter, for example, was buying employer and candidate traffic on a pay-for-performance basis through its affiliate program in 1998. Within months, one of the world's largest hospitality companies was paying us $0.05 per click in return for driving thousands of students and recent graduates a month to apply at the employer's website. This employer, and others like it, seemingly recognized the value of receiving resume data electronically and being able to automatically and accurately track the source of those applications. "You can't manage what you can't measure", is a mantra that marketing experts embrace. Yet few employers today seem to have the inclination to properly track the sources of candidates who visit the employer's career site let alone those who apply, are interviewed, get hired, and prove to be top performers.

Today, a large majority of employers with more than 1,000 employees, and even many of those which are far smaller, use ATS from vendors such as Taleo and iCIMS. In an effort to provide a better experience for both the candidate and recruiter, some of these employers have added on front-end technology from vendors such as Jibe, Smashfly, and Successfactors. The almost universal adoption of sophisticated and very expensive software has enabled employers to more efficiently manage the flow of candidates into and through their recruiting functions. Indeed, you'd be hard pressed to find an ATS or front-end software offering which does not allow employers to track the source of click, application, and even hire back to a job board, school, career fair, third-party recruiter, or other sources for the candidate. One might think that's a good thing as we're now able to measure and therefore manage how we're sourcing our hires. Yet these software systems all share two inherent flaws, one of which is related to technology and the second of which appears to be a deliberate disregard for how recruiting really works.

Technology flaws inherent in tracking systems used by employers

Let's first tackle the issue of the technology flaws. Almost all of these systems rely upon the employer providing to the source a code to add to the beginning (prepend) or end (append) or the web page (URL) to which the source sends the candidate. Requesting these codes from our direct employer customers is part of the formal, documented, step-by-step process followed by College Recruiter. Based upon my conversations with executives at other general, aggregators, and niche job boards, I suspect that almost all of the other well known, high traffic sites also request these codes. However, from conversations that I've had with executives of smaller sites and career service office leaders, few of those request these codes and many of them are unaware they even exist.

Let's also keep in mind that there's a difference between a request and a receipt. Even though we request the tracking codes, only about half of our employer customer contacts both know how to generate a source tracking code AND use them when posting jobs to our site. Undoubtedly that knowledge exists within their organizations but if the recruiter who posts the job doesn't know how to generate the code, or isn't inclined to do so for whatever reason, then the technology might as well not exist.

But let's assume that the recruiter is well versed on the intricacies of their employer's software and is diligent in using the source tracking codes. Do they even work? The answer, sadly, is only sometimes. Why? Because the code prepended or appended to a URL typically only work if the candidate clicks through to the employer's site and immediately starts and, with many of these systems, also completes the application. Think about how the vast majority of employer websites require candidates to enter data into dozens and sometimes hundreds of fields such as first name, last name, street address, city, state/province, country, postal code, phone number, job titles, dates of employment, schools, majors, years of graduation, and then, and here's the kicker, upload a resume. Do you have your resume saved on your phone? Even if you did, would you know how to navigate your phone's memory to then upload that file to an ATS? So candidates using their phones or tablets to search for jobs and find one of yours will likely hit the proverbial brick wall when they try to apply. No matter how thoughtful you and your vendors have been and how much of your budget you've allocated to making the mobile experience as painless as possible, it is still painful and candidates are likely to abandon their efforts before they start and almost certainly before they finish applying.

Candidates who use a mobile device and find your opportunity on a job board, career service office website, or elsewhere may look at your ad but when they're ready to apply — and that may be hours, days, or even weeks after they first see your ad — will likely hop over to their laptop or desktop computer. Many and perhaps most of the largest, most sophisticated employers refuse to acknowledge that their entire system of tracking their sources of hire is based upon the flawed assumption that the vast majority of candidates see an ad, click, and apply. That's never been true and is less true today than ever before. By 2014, Facebook announced that almost half of adults accessed the Internet each day using two devices and a third used three or more.

Put yourself in the shoes of the typical students who may be interested in your opportunity. They're likely to use their mobile device to find a job opportunity on a job board, career service office website, or elsewhere. But they're unlikely to apply using that device and also unlikely to hop onto their laptop or desktop, go back to the job board or other site, re-run their search to try to find the job posting, and then click through to your ATS apply. They're far more likely to use their mobile to find your job, make a mental note to later use their laptop or desktop to apply, later hop over to their laptop or desktop, and go to your site directly to apply. And, if they do that, they're not clicking through that trackable URL and so you probably won't get accurate data on the source of the click, application, or hire.

Some of our employer customers have attempted to get around this problem by adding an additional layer of tracking. Vendors such as Doubleclick, which is owned by Google, can provide you with tracking pixel codes that you or your media partner add to your job posting ads. You can add the hidden code to your ads on most of the larger job boards but not to those on many of the career service office sites and smaller job boards. But aside from the inherent problem of tracking your clicks, applications, and hires from only some of your sources, there are other problems. The way that this additional layer of tracking works is by dropping a small file — a cookie — onto the candidate's computer. The cookie contains information about where the ad was seen and therefore allows these vendors to report to you that a candidate saw your ad one day and came back directly to your site hours, days, or even weeks later to apply even if they didn't click the trackable URL. Some of these vendors, including Doubleclick/Google, have such massive data on virtually all Internet users that the vendors can know that a user who saw your ad on one of their devices but then went to your site directly from another of their devices is the same person. You'll then be able to track that click, application, or hire made on one device back to the user who was on a different device when they first read your job posting ad. Pretty slick, huh? Except there are flaws.

First, let's assume that the user's mobile device accepts cookies. Many don't. Let's also assume that the user is not reading your ad on a browser that allows cookies to be dropped. Apps and some of the most popular browsers such as Safari reject cookies. If we get past those hurdles and you're able to drop a cookie onto the user's mobile device then you'd think that Doubleclick/Google and other, somewhat similar services will now correlate the user's mobile device with their laptop or desktop. In theory, yes. In practice, often not. Studies show that Doubleclick/Google is often unable to properly attribute an application started on a mobile device and completed on a desktop computer even when the candidate's device and browser accept cookies. The true source — the site that referred the candidate to your mobile site — often gets lost and that destroys your ability to properly attribute your sources of hire let alone your sources of applications and clicks.

The automated tracking systems which are cookie-based are well designed for tracking the kind of traffic we saw in the 1990's and 2000's, which was from websites. Although every major web browser including Chrome, Firefox, Safari, and Internet Explorer allow the user to block cookies, very few users even know what a cookie is let alone know how to block them or would even care to block them. However, most Internet traffic today is mobile and there's a big, big difference between web and mobile traffic. A sizable and rapidly increasing share of mobile traffic is from devices and through applications and mobile browsers which, by default, reject all cookies. There's a good likelihood that you will not be able to accurately track the source of the application from the candidate who sees your job posting ad on a job board, career service office site, or other sites but does not apply until they hop over to their laptop or desktop.

Attribution to one source is illogical

And now to the second and perhaps even more significant problem: attributing a click, application, or hire to one source is illogical. Think about any significant decision that you've ever made. Did you ever rely upon one piece of information to make that decision when other, credible sources of information were easily accessible? When you applied to your current job, did you only consider the information that you received on the job board where you first learned of the opportunity, or only the information from your friend who worked for the employer, or only the "we're hiring" billboard outside of what is now your place of employment? Hopefully not. Significant decisions in life tend to and should be influenced by multiple data points. Yes, you first learned of the job through an ad on a job board. But before you even clicked to apply, you hopped over to Google and ran a few searches to find out more about the employer. Those searches led you to Glassdoor, LinkedIn, and some other sites. You then talked to a few friends and family members. And then maybe you went back to the job board but probably you went straight to the employer's career site to apply. Is the job board your source of hire? Google? Glassdoor? LinkedIn? A referral? And don't even get me started about how career sites cannot be sources of hire as no one ever started their job search at a career site so, at best, they're a destination and not a source of hire.

The reality is that every candidate for every position has multiple sources of hire. So even if your technology claims to be able to attribute the application and hire to a source, is it THE source? Is there even such a thing as "the" source? Many talent acquisition leaders acknowledge that there is no such thing as a single source of hire yet claim that using flawed data is better than using no data. I'm not so sure. Over time, I've come to realize that we need to stop pretending that there is only one source per hire. I get that we do so because some of the most popular tracking software only allows for that option. But those products force us into improperly measuring and managing the allocation of our marketing resources and so their very design makes it unwise to rely upon such products.

The solution: We need to adjust our thinking

We're at a tipping point. We're actually a little past the tipping point. The tipping point occurred a couple of years ago when the amount of mobile Internet traffic from phones and tablets first exceeded the web traffic from laptops and desktops. Despite the advances in technology, we're now less able to accurately track the sources of our applications, hires, and star performers.

And even if we could accurately track to a source, it would be intellectually dishonest for us to do so. So, what's the solution? I believe that we all need to step back, reconsider what we're trying to measure and why, and adjust our thinking.

We're trying to measure the source of hire so that we can properly allocate our limited staff time and marketing budgets, right? Bringing accountability into any business process is a good idea but is it correct to hold your job board, career service office, and other partners accountable for whether a candidate was hired? It seems to me that people and organizations should be held accountable for outcomes which are largely within their control and neither rewarded nor punished for outcomes which are largely outside of their control. If an employee is with your organization for a decade, should the person who hired and managed them during their internship be held accountable for the employee's work performance in their tenth year with your organization? Few would argue that the hiring manager in that scenario should be held accountable for the employee's work performance much beyond their internship.

Let's take another step. Should the recruiter who reviewed 50 applications and narrowed the candidates to the best three be held accountable for the work performance of the candidate? Most talent acquisition leaders say yes. But what if the hiring manager rejected the three finalists and instead selected his niece? Few talent acquisition leaders would then hold the recruiter accountable for the work performance of the niece, whether her performance was sterling or abysmal. And what about the recruiter who brought three candidates to the hiring manager, all three candidates met all of the requirements and preferences communicated to the recruiter by the hiring manager, one of the candidates was hired, but then the new employee was poorly managed? Is the likely unsatisfactory work performance of that employee a reflection on the work of the recruiter or the hiring manager? Again, few would argue that the recruiter in that scenario should be accountable for the employee's work performance. The recruiters' responsibility — and therefore what they should be accountable for — ended when they presented the qualified candidates to the hiring manager.

Ready for the next step? Why do we hold career service offices, job boards, and other partners accountable for the number of candidates we source from them and therefore measure them based upon their cost-per-hire? This metric has become key to talent acquisition leaders who are trying to evaluate their sources of hire yet, I argue, it is an incredibly poor metric. A typical Fortune 1,000 company or federal government agency with a college recruiting program visits multiple and sometimes dozens or even hundreds of college campuses and advertises their job openings on a number of job boards and other websites. An increasing number of employers are using tools ranging from Excel spreadsheets to software-as-a-service products such as Yello and WCN to track the number of clicks, applications, and hires as well as the related expenses to each of these sources. They're measuring in an effort to better manage and I applaud them for those efforts.

If a recruiter delivers hundreds of outstanding candidates to her hiring managers and those hiring managers fail to hire any, is that a reflection upon the work performance of the recruiter or the hiring manager? Given that the decision about how many to hire and who to hire lays with the hiring manager and not the recruiter, shouldn't the hiring manager be held accountable for the hiring and not the recruiter? Similarly, if a school delivers to a recruiter a dozen outstanding candidates and the recruiter fails to follow through, shouldn't it be the recruiter and not the school who is held accountable? And if that makes sense, then doesn't it also make sense that if the job board or other media partner delivers outstanding candidates and the recruiter fails to follow through, shouldn't it be the recruiter and not the media partner who is held accountable? If that's all true, then why are we measuring the performance of schools and media partners by cost-per-hire?

An increasing number of employers are hiring an increasing number of candidates through what many now refer to as "virtual" recruitment efforts, meaning through job boards and other on-line initiatives. Most on-line traffic is now mobile and most of that traffic cannot be accurately tracked back to the source. If ever there was a time for employers to re-think how they're evaluating their sources of hiring, that time is now. The manager of an employee who has been with an employer for a decade should be rewarded and otherwise held accountable for the work performance of that employee and not the hiring manager, recruiter, career service office, or job board. The hiring manager of an intern should be rewarded and otherwise held accountable for the work performance of that intern and not the recruiter, career service office, or job board. The recruiter of an intern should be rewarded and otherwise held accountable for presenting to the hiring manager well qualified applicants and not the career service office or job board. And career service offices and job boards should be rewarded and otherwise held accountable only for delivering to the recruiter well targeted applicants Why? Because we are not involved in screening applicants and therefore should not be held accountable for which applicants are qualified versus merely well targeted.

So, let's break down that last link in the chain: How recruiters should hold accountable their career service, job board, and other partners. If it is the job of the recruiter is to screen and therefore determine which applicants are qualified, then it is the recruiter who is largely within control of determining which applicants are qualified and not the career service office, job board, or other partners. That means that, at best, the career service office, job board, or other partner should be held accountable for the number of well targeted students and recent graduates that they deliver to the employer. Unlike in the 1980's and even into the 1990's when that delivery took the form of a printed or faxed resume, today that delivery typically takes the form of a click to the employer's website or online application. If an employer spends thousands to tens of thousands of dollars visiting a college campus or hundreds to thousands of dollars advertising their jobs online, that employer should be able to articulate to the school, job board, or other partner what education, experience, diversity, and other attributes the employer wants to see in candidates. It is then up to the school, job board, or other source to deliver those candidates to the employer whether that means to an on-campus information session, career fair, online application, or click to the employer's website. Those tasks are largely within the control of the source and therefore the source should be held accountable for those tasks. Nothing more and nothing less.

Does this approach mean that employers should ignore the quality of the candidates when determining where to invest their time, money, and other resources? Hardly. An employer who visits a college campus to hire five electrical engineers and finds that the career service office allowed any student to register for the interviews and so most of the interviews were with fine arts majors is an employer who should choose to visit another college campus during their next hiring cycle. An employer who advertises a job opening for a registered nurse in Houston and whose job board partner drives thousands of clicks from administrative and clerical candidates in Los Angeles is an employer who should choose to use a different job board during their next hiring cycle. College career service offices, job boards, and other sources should and must be rewarded and otherwise held accountable for what is largely within their control: driving well targeted students and recent graduates to the application process favored by the employer.

So now to the $800 question: How should an employer evaluate the performance of one career service office against another, one job board against another, and even one career service office against a job board? Both the Society for Human Resource Management (SHRM) and the National Association of Colleges and Employers (NACE) advocate for employers to include all of their costs of recruiting when measuring their costs-per-hire. By extension, that means that employers should include all of their recruiting costs when measuring their costs-per-application and costs-per-click. These measures, of course, look only at the cost side of the equation and not the value delivered to the employer by the work performance of the employee but let's cross that bridge a little later. Employers are often astounded at how much more or less expensive their sources are when those employers start to properly include in their costs. Those costs are not just the checks that they write to a school, job board, or other source but also the full cost of the staff time required to engage with that source. Some sources that require little out-of-pocket investment prove to the very expensive when staff time is taken into account, and other sources that seemed to be frightfully expensive prove to be bargains when the employer realizes that their biggest real cost was writing a check and that little staff time was required to deliver many well targeted candidates.

Years ago, I was fortunate to sit in on a presentation delivered at a recruiting conference by a talent acquisition leader for a large, healthcare provider. The presenter pulled up a slide that showed the cost-per-click, cost-per-application, cost-per-interview, and cost-per-hire for dozens of her sources. The most expensive source on a per hire basis was a big, general job board. The least expensive sources were niche job boards. Why, I asked myself, would such as smart talent acquisition leader brag about spending so much money on such an expensive source? Before I had the chance to ask, she addressed the question head-on. If she could hire every physical therapist, occupational therapist, nurse, and other employee through niche job boards then she would stop advertising on the general job board. But the niche job boards were not delivering the number of well targeted applicants the employer needed, and so the employer continued to use the general job board.

Recent conversations that I've had with some of the wisest talent acquisition leaders in the college recruiting space have led me to understand that they're making similar calculations about where and how to source their applicants. If they could get enough from the lowest cost source — school, job board, or other — they would. But they can't and so they spread their resources around. My hope is that, over time, they will better allocate those resources based upon the outcomes those resources deliver, both in terms of cost and value.

Which brings us to the other side of the equation: value. It is one thing to minimize your cost-per-hire or even cost-per-applicant. It is another to recruit and retain star performers. Many talent acquisition leaders have absolutely no window into the performance of those they hired. They typically don't know who is still with the company even a year after their start date let alone know who is performing admirably and who needs to find another place of employment. Does your organization track the work performance of its employees? And if you're the rare employer who does, do you hold your managers and not your sources accountable for that performance? Remember, career service offices, job boards, and other sources are not involved in selecting which candidates you deem to be well qualified nor do they extend offers, hire, onboard, train, or manage. So, when you hold your sources accountable, hold them accountable for what is largely within their control — delivering well targeted candidates into your recruiting process — and not what is largely outside of their control — how many are interviewed, offered jobs, hired, and perform well.

References:

Bialecki, A. (2016). Tracking Email Conversions in 2016: Pixels and Cookies Aren't Enough. Retrieved from: https://www.klaviyo.com/blog/tracking-email-conversions-in-2016-pixels-and-cookies-arent-enough.

Johannes (2016). 3 Biggest Mobile Ad Tracking Pitfalls Explained & How to Avoid Them. Retrieved from: https://medium.com/@Daimo/3-biggest-mobile-ad-tracking-pitfalls-explained-how-to-avoid-them-c38f9b8bfb9#.3dnzrty57

Lella, A. (2015). Number of Mobile-Only Internet Users Now Exceeds Desktop-Only Users in the U.S. Retrieved from: https://www.comscore.com/Insights/Blog/Number-of-Mobile-Only-Internet-Users-Now-Exceeds-Desktop-Only-in-the-U.S

Rothberg, S. (2010). Employers: Your Career Sites Are Not Sources of Hire. Retrieved from: https://www.collegerecruiter.com/blog/2010/02/17/employers-your-career-sites-are-not-sources-of-hires-2/

Executive Leadership – Driving Campus Engagement from the C-Suite: An Interview with Charlie Chasin

Susan K. Reid

What is the cornerstone of an effective campus-corporate partnership? Ideally, it features a level of executive leadership and involvement. Charlie Chasin, Managing Director and Head of Reengineering and Expense Management at Morgan Stanley, exemplifies both that leadership and involvement. Charlie has led the campus recruiting efforts for Morgan Stanley at New York University (NYU) for more than a decade, and each year helps bring several dozen talented summer and full-time analysts and associates to the Firm.

As Managing Director and Global Head of Diversity and Inclusion at Morgan Stanley, I interviewed Charlie to better understand his long-standing relationship with NYU and his commitment to driving an effective campus-corporate relationship.

Charlie Chasin is a Managing Director of Morgan Stanley and the Global Head of Reengineering and Expense Management. He has run the Firm's global expense management effort since 2009. Over the past 28 years, Mr. Chasin has held numerous positions at Morgan Stanley, including Chief Operating Officer of the Finance Division, Senior Business Risk Officer for Morgan Stanley Bank, Chief of Staff to two of the Firm's presidents, Legal & Regulatory Risk Manager for the Fixed Income Division and Global Head of Litigation & Regulatory Affairs. Before joining Morgan Stanley, Mr. Chasin was a litigator at Dewey, Ballantine, Bushby, Palmer & Wood, an Adjunct Professor of Business Law at NYU Stern and a law clerk to US District Judge John Bartels (EDNY). Mr. Chasin graduated magna cum laude from NYU's College of Business and Public Administration in 1980 with a BS in Accounting, and received his JD from NYU Law School in 1983, where he was a member of the Law Review.

How did you become involved with the career center at NYU?

I attended NYU as an undergraduate in the late 1970's and fondly remember working as a student on campus. I had the enviable job of making ID cards. Back then, the process was quite manual. I took student photos with a Polaroid camera, cut them to size, inserted them into plastic sleeves, sealed them and typed the student's name and social security number, which served as the ID number in pre-identity theft days, onto the ID card with an embossing machine. I worked for a staff member in the Admissions Office at the time, and she was so much more than a supervisor. She took me under her wing and connected me to the career center, which in turn helped me to clarify my career goals. I eventually made my way to NYU Law School and ultimately a career in financial services.

What impact did career services have on your career?

After visiting the career center, I landed a summer job doing accounting work at a medium-sized law firm. I originally thought I wanted a career in accounting. As the oldest child of a widowed mom, my goal then was to get a stable job, and I thought accounting would provide that. But thanks to career services, after a summer of working at a law firm, I decided to go to law school. Like a lot of students who finally make their way there, I found career services to be very helpful. Without their guidance and support, I would not have made an informed career choice.

How and why did you come to take on the role of executive champion for NYU?

I received two degrees from NYU, my undergraduate degree and my law degree, and I've been actively involved in various alumni efforts in support of the school. Fifteen years ago, I took on the role of captain for Morgan Stanley's Fixed Income Division NYU recruiting team, and thereafter was asked to serve as Morgan Stanley's University Relationship Manager for NYU. Those responsibilities of course gave me the opportunity to work closely with the leadership team at the NYU Wasserman Center for Career Services. They were welcoming, engaging, and responsive. I found myself quickly immersed in expanding the relationship between Morgan Stanley and the university.

Over the years, I've had the opportunity to work with various deans at the Stern School of Business, The College of Arts and Sciences, and the Law

School as well as many of their terrific colleagues and staff. I've also had the opportunity to work with the Office of the President. Those relationships contribute directly to our firm-wide success and helped cement my desire to advance our relationship with the university across multiple dimensions.

What role should Career Services play in developing talent for the corporate world?

Schools have not always done enough to prepare students for the corporate world. Career services should be involved more aggressively in the process of helping students think about what they might want to do and where they might want to go after graduation. Students need to think about this early on to help them make good career choices and, along with their faculty, career services professionals can help them best make those important decisions. The cost of education is high and it's important to think about career choices early to ensure a good return on the significant investment made in attending college.

What are you looking for in talent coming from colleges and universities?

Morgan Stanley is fortunate to have many smart, accomplished people applying for great entry-level positions at our firm. Everyone focuses on different things but my personal focus has always been on ethics, integrity and cultural fit. Candidates who tend to succeed in the long run at Morgan Stanley are smart, hard-working, driven, innovative, strategic, tactical, collegial and true team players.

Much has been written about millennials. Do you see marked differences between millennials and other generations?

I went to school in the 1970's and 1980's and felt lucky to get a job. On the plus side, millennials have greater clarity about their career goals than we did, and they expect greater work-life balance. But many people also perceive millennials as impatient with respect to career advancement (promotion and pay). Some of this impatience is fueled in part by a culture that celebrates the "millionaire/billionaire" entrepreneur phenomenon, which sometimes affects their expectations.

How should career services change to meet the needs of millennials?

Career services should become involved with students earlier and build a longer-term relationship with students. In addition, career services should build partnerships with academic advisors to help advise students on a longer-term basis as millennials navigate college. Of course, they should develop meaningful working relationships with hiring organizations to ensure that their students have the broadest possible array of potential high-quality employment opportunities.

What about employers? How can career services help employers prepare to meet the needs of millennials?

Career services is crucial to this! In my case, I built a great rapport with the leadership of Career Services at NYU and they have been instrumental to helping us identify talent. This include the "obviously talented" but also the "diamonds in the rough." We are able to go to NYU to talk with students and we sponsor the Morgan Stanley Boot Camp series, which includes Business Boot Camp for Liberal Arts Majors. Programs such as this helps us to get to know and understand students better and to identify talent early. Many career services professionals have strong relationships with students and can talk about candidates more candidly and help focus employers on the unique experiences of students that can imply a good fit.

Diversity is a key focus for employers. How can career services help here?

Career services can help in a number of ways. They can host diversity events to help connect employers and students, and they can identify and introduce appropriate diversity candidates to employers. Close connections help; the more events we do informally, the better we get to know students and, again, career services can help facilitate these important connections. The funnel and talent pipeline has to be full to yield diversity and career services is a critical partner here so it's important to have a strong relationship.

What do you see as the key elements of a strong relationship between career services and corporations?

Develop a deep and trusted relationship. I have a strong relationship with

NYU and I prioritize my relationship with the talented team at the Wasserman Center. And I'm supportive with time and resources, which is important to the success of career services. In turn, career services should pursue relationships with executives by asking for their involvement and help. Be direct about what what you need and, most importantly, be creative in figuring out ways you can work together.

Author Biographies

Adrienne Alberts

Adrienne Alberts, Director, Talent Acquisition Programs and Operations, for the American Red Cross, has been involved in talent management and career development for nearly 20 years. In her current role, she manages organization-wide talent acquisition programs (college and diversity recruiting), vendor relationships, and strategic sourcing efforts. Prior to joining the Red Cross, Adrienne managed college relations for Booz Allen Hamilton, and college and diversity recruiting for Constellation Energy Group. Adrienne has also served as the director of client services for MonsterTrak, a division of Monster Worldwide, and on the staffs of career centers at Johns Hopkins University, the University of Virginia, and the College of William and Mary.

Adrienne is member of the National Association of Colleges and Employers board of directors and a past President for the Eastern Association of Colleges and Employers. She serves on the board of the Sellinger School of Business at Loyola University in Maryland and is Vice President of the Caroline Center Board of Directors. The Caroline Center is a non-profit organization focusing on career preparation for unemployed and underemployed women in Baltimore City. Adrienne has also served on the boards of the Maryland Career Consortium, the Professional Aptitude Council, Owen Software Development Company, Ltd, and University of Richmond Office of Alumni and Career Services and the University of Maryland University Career Services and The President's Promise.

Led by her passion to make an impact, Adrienne founded Alberts Consulting LLC in 2010. Alberts Consulting is a small consulting firm that focuses on coaching for individuals and training and strategy development for organizations. Adrienne has diverse experience in career development, diversity recruiting, effective service delivery, and process improvement. A native of Virginia, she received her M.Ed. in Counseling Psychology with a concentration on College Student Personnel Administration and her B.S. in Psychology from James Madison University in Harrisonburg, VA.

Dan Black

Dan is the Americas Recruiting Leader for EY, a global leader in assurance, tax, transaction and advisory services. Dan leads a team of executive, experienced and campus recruiters in solidifying EY member firms' market leadership position as an employer of choice in North and South America. He is also actively involved in developing EY's global talent acquisition strategy and regularly consults with EY clients on their recruitment and employer brand strategies. Additionally, Dan is a past president and longtime board member of the National Association of Colleges and Employers (NACE), the leading US organization focused on the employment of the college educated.

With nearly 20 years of recruiting expertise, Dan is a highly sought after speaker who frequently provides insights on recruiting trends and is a passionate advocate on behalf of Millennials. Dan regularly provides commentary through leading media outlets such as the *Wall Street Journal, CNN, National Public Radio, CBS Radio, FORTUNE, Forbes, Fox Business,* and *the New York Times,* among others. He has served as a keynote speaker at universities, conferences, and industry events around the world. He is active in numerous professional and academic organizations, including regular involvement with his alma maters, Binghamton University and Fordham University. Dan is very active in his community and in philanthropic organizations.

He serves as a Corporate Advisory Board member for the March of Dimes, ranking among its top 100 US fundraisers for the past seven years. Additionally, Dan is a volunteer firefighter and Treasurer for the Archville Fire Department and is a Board Member for the Tarrytown/Sleepy Hollow American Youth Soccer Organization.

Thomas Borgerding

Thomas is the President/CEO of Campus Media Group, a consulting, marketing and advertising agency helping employers and brands confidently engage college students through experiential events, digital marketing, content marketing, and on campus marketing. Thomas has been passionate about helping employers reach and engage their best candidates since 1996. He's been a speaker at NACE and SHRM. He also founded the Minnesota Interactive Marketing Association.

Helen Brown

Helen Brown has been with Vector Marketing since June of 1991, when she was recruited as a sales representative while attending Indiana University of Pennsylvania (IUP). After graduating with a Bachelor's Degree in International Studies two years later, she invested further into Vector and, inevitably, into herself. She developed skills and was promoted to Branch Manager and would lead her to a three-year long role as District Manager in Pennsylvania and Massachusetts. In October of 2001, Helen was promoted to Northeast Region Campus Relations Manager, making her responsible for establishing and building positive recruiting relationships with colleges throughout the Northeast region.

In July of 2011, she was promoted to National Campus Recruiting Manager and quickly followed up with another promotion on August 1, 2012 to her current position as Academic Outreach Manager. She now oversees campus recruiting, academic philanthropies, Cutco® in the Classroom program, and an Academic Advisory Board in the U.S. and Canada. As former Treasurer and President for the Eastern Association of Colleges and Employers (EACE) and former Co-Chair of the Principles of Committee for National Association of Colleges and Employers, Helen has developed a deep appreciation for her job that has allowed her to travel across the United States and work with students and managers to further develop recruiting programs.

As you'll find on her personal blog, TravelWithLaughter.com, Helen is also passionate about photography and surrounding herself with friends and family.

Christopher Carlson

Based in Chattanooga, Christopher is the Director of Talent Acquisition and Diversity for the Tennessee Valley Authority. He leads a team of professionals focused on delivering best-in-class recruitment and diversity solutions. Prior to TVA, he was Senior Manager of Talent Acquisition for Booz Allen Hamilton where for over ten years he oversaw a variety of talent acquisition programs including university, diversity, military, employee referral programs.

He is active with the National Association of Colleges and Employers serving as the Vice President, Employers currently and has held positions on the2012-2014 NACE Board of Directors, co-chair for a number of committees including the Career Readiness committee in 2014-2016 and has presented at a variety of conference workshops on both university and diversity topics. He serves on the Board for the Urban League of Chattanooga and previously the USBLN Industrial Advisory Board.

Christopher has held a number of recruiting and consulting roles within the consulting, entertainment, and non-for-profit industries. He holds a bachelor's degree in psychology from Virginia Commonwealth University and is currently pursuing a MPA from Florida Tech.

Dustin Clinard

As Managing Director for the Americas at Universum Global, Dustin gets extremely excited about the data-led, human, and purposeful strategy Universum deploys in the field of employer branding, bringing logic to chaos and passion with a purpose. Dustin is responsible for Universum's teams covering North and South America, including client growth, new client acquisition, and delivery functions.

Prior to Universum, Dustin has held senior leadership roles for the Institute for Corporate Productivity (i4cp), Mind Gym, Corporate Executive Board (CEB), and BASF. He has improved chemical plant productivity, consulted to some of the world's biggest and best companies, and expanded businesses from one continent to another. Dustin has his BS in Chemical Engineering from the University of Michigan and his MBA from Northwestern's Kellogg School of Management.

Emanuel "Manny" Contomanolis

Manny is Senior Associate Vice President for Enrollment Management and Career Services and Director of the Office of Career Services and Cooperative Education at the Rochester Institute of Technology. He has more than 35 years of higher education experience and is active as a consultant, speaker and writer.

Manny is a past president of the National Association of Colleges and Employers (NACE) and is a member of the NACE Academy of Fellows as well as a recipient of the NACE Kauffman Award for outstanding contributions to the field. He is active in a number of national benchmarking groups and is a frequent media contributor.

Manny has a PhD in higher education leadership and administration from the University of Buffalo, an MA in College Student Personnel from Bowling Green State University, and a graduate certificate in industrial and labor relations from Cornell University.

Caroline Cunningham

Caroline Cunningham is currently the Director of University Relations and Diversity Programs at GE Digital where she has been for the past year. She has 17+ years of staffing experience and has worked in a variety of industries including oil and gas, healthcare, consumer distribution and non-profit services. Just prior to coming to GE she was the Team Leader, Enterprise Hiring for Chevron Corporation where she was responsible for U.S university recruiting and enterprise intern programs as well as petrotech sourcing for both university and experienced hiring. Her team also served as a center of excellence for global process and program consulting. Caroline was with Chevron since 2007 where she worked in several similar progressive roles throughout HR Shared Services, University Affairs and Enterprise Hiring. Prior to joining Chevron, she spent six years at Johnson & Johnson in pharmaceutical manufacturing where she managed both university and experienced hiring.

Caroline is an active member of NACE (National Association of Colleges and Employers) and is currently serving a two-year term on the board of directors as an Employer Director. Over the past ten years she has participated on and led numerous committees and was the co-chair for the 2015 National Conference. She has presented at several national and regional conferences and events on a variety of topics related to recruiting and talent acquisition. She holds a bachelor's degree in theater arts from Occidental College and both a PHR (Professional in Human Resources) and SHRM-CPC Certification.

John Flato

John is the Vice President of Advisory Services at Universum Global, an employer branding firm. In this role, he advises partner clients on the design, implementation and improvement of their campus recruiting and relations efforts as well as providing a variety of marketing and branding activities with undergraduate and MBA schools for Universum. John has directed the campus recruiting programs at three organizations, and has won numerous awards from the National Association of Colleges and Employers and the Employment Management Association for creative recruiting materials, technical innovation, and educational programming. He has also served as the Director of Career Management at Georgetown University's MBA School and taught Human Resources in The Johns Hopkins University graduate business program. He is a frequent speaker, published chapters in three books in Human Resources, and has been quoted in the media on a variety of campus recruiting issues.

Glen Fowler

Glen is the Recruiting and Training Manager with the California State Auditor's Office. The office is the State's independent external auditor that reports to the California Legislature and provides nonpartisan, accurate, and timely assessments of California government's financial and operational activities. Currently, Glen is the National Association of Colleges and Employers 2016-17 President Elect. Also, he serves as the Chairperson for the National State Auditors Association's (NSAA) Training Committee, and he serves on the NSAA's Human Resources Committee.

Previously, Glen served as President for the Mountain Pacific Association of Colleges and Employers with his term ending June 2011, and he was the recipient of the "Outstanding Service Award" in 2012. Similarly, at the California State Auditor's Office Glen was the recipient of the "State Auditor's Award", the "Team Player Award", and the "Best Place to Launch a Career Award".

Glen received his Bachelor's Degree from the University of California, Berkeley, in 1986, and his Master's degree from the California State

University, Sacramento, in 1989.

Valerie Berger Fred

Valerie is a Vice President in Human Resources at Macquarie and has over 15 years of experience in Campus Recruitment related activities. She joined Macquarie in 2010 to run the US Campus Recruiting efforts for the firm. Prior to joining Macquarie, Valerie held a variety of roles including: Campus Recruiting Manager for Goldman Sachs and Senior Relationship Manager in NYU Stern's MBA Office of Career Development. Valerie earned a Bachelor of Arts degree from Lehigh University.

Aaron Goldberg

Aaron is Citi's University Relations and Campus Diversity Manager and has worked at Citi since March 2014. Prior to becoming University Relations and Campus Diversity Manager, Aaron worked as Citi's Campus Recruiter and Program Manager for the Global Engagement Management Associate (GEMA) and Compliance Associate Programs. Based in New York, Aaron's role involves working with Citi's university partners to ensure the firm has strong pipelines to top talent nationwide. He also spends significant time on-campus working with students to help prepare them for the recruiting process.

Prior to joining Citi, Aaron worked in several capacities for Masa Israel, a project of the Prime Minister's Office of the Government of Israel, where he connected talented young adults to internships and professional development opportunities within the Israeli economy. Aaron graduated with a B.A. in International Relations from James Madison University.

Diana Gruverman

With over 15 years of experience in university relations and career development, Diana's passion is helping college students achieve their career goals. As the Americas Team Lead for Campus Recruiting at AIG, she develops a firm-wide campus recruiting strategy that engages business partners and school partners to identify full-time and intern talent for entry-level pipeline programs at AIG. Diana ensures positive outcomes by executing strategic planning, dynamic programming, and creative solutions to engage junior talent.

Prior to joining AIG, Diana was the Senior Director at the NYU Wasserman Center for Career Development where she oversaw strategic operations and employer engagement. She developed relationships with recruiters and hiring managers across industries and helped design recruitment and branding strategies to ensure a solid pipeline of talent to meet the hiring goals of each organization. Diana's input on the labor market, job search strategies, employer engagement, and campus recruiting has been shared in media outlets such as AM New York, Chronicle of Higher Education, LinkedIn, Metro, New York Post, Village Voice, WABC TV, WetFeet, among others. She also presents on panels and at national conferences.

Diana has a MA in Industrial/Organizational Psychology from NYU and a BA in Psychology from the University of Pennsylvania.

Ren Herring

Ren is a Campus Talent Acquisition Manager at PwC, one of the world's largest professional services firms. Prior to joining PwC, Ren worked extensively in student and professional development when at both NYU's School of Professional Studies and College of Arts and Science. Ren holds an MA in higher education and student affairs from NYU and a BS in business administration from California State University Monterey Bay.

Morgan Hoogvelt

Morgan is a career Talent Acquisition expert serving in multiple capacities such as Executive Search Recruiter, Fortune 500 Talent Acquisition leader and Search Firm proprietor. Drawing on his expertise in human capital strategy, executive search, RPO, essential hiring practices, candidate sourcing, Internet recruiting, and social networking, he provides organizations targeted, best-of-class solutions and employment branding strategies that help his clients meet the challenges of recruiting, technology, and retaining and rewarding top talent. He is also passionate about delivering excellent customer service and building positive, productive relationships. Prior to his career within Corporate America; Morgan served in the U.S. Navy

Ripp Kardon

Since graduating from the College of Charleston, Ripp has reveled in his career - finding great talent while incorporating significant amounts of shenanigans and laughter. From small tech to Fortune 200 companies Ripp has recruited for every level and (almost) every type of talent. The last four years Ripp has been enamored and focused in Campus Recruiting and he could not be more thankful for finding his passion. Always learning, always asking and always looking for ways to do it better, faster, stronger and with more ROI.

A proud graduate of the NACE's Leadership Advancement Program and currently serving on his third committee. Ripp leads Campus Recruiting for Belk Department Stores in Charlotte, NC and loves identifying talent and building programs that will help change the face of retail. Ripp was born in Tangier, Morocco and moved to Philadelphia where his unwavering deep love for Philadelphia began. He has resided in Charlotte, NC since 2014.

Katharine Lynn

Kat joined Universum in 2012 as a project manager for Universum's annual *Most Attractive Employers* supplement, negotiating placement in the Wall Street Journey and helping corporate clients brand themselves to their target talent. She managed the marketing for Universum Americas for several years, including the Employer Branding Conference and annual Most Attractive Employer rankings. Prior to joining Universum, Kat attended Georgetown University where she graduated with a degree in English. She is currently a Project Manager in Site Reliability Operations for Palantir Technologies.

Marilyn Mackes

Marilyn is the Executive Director of the National Association of Colleges and Employers (NACE), leading an organization of over 3,000 employing organizations and educational institutions with 11,550 individuals engaged in the career development and employment process of college students and alumni.

In her extensive interactions with employment recruiting professionals as well as leaders in business, government, education and the media, Marilyn addresses issues such as employment and salary trends, benchmarking for effective recruiting strategies and best practices in career development and hiring, building a diverse workforce, global recruitment strategies, leveraging technology for recruitment, and candidate and employer expectations.

Marilyn has been a consultant and trainer in the college relations and recruiting field for more than 20 years and has presented to various professional, business and government organizations in the United States and abroad. She regularly conducts media interviews regarding the college employment market and has appeared on ABC Nightly News, CNN Headline News, MSNBC, CBS and The NewsHour.

Marilyn is a member of the Council of Human Resource Management Associations (COHRMA) and the Council of Higher Education Management Associations (CHEMA). Prior to assuming her role at NACE, Marilyn received her PhD from Lehigh University and held a variety of executive and academic positions in higher education.

Laura Mills

Laura Mills currently works as a Faculty Relations Consultant in EY's University Relations group. Her work takes her all over the country to liaison with faculty and administrators at colleges and universities seeking to partner with EY for recruiting, funding & research. Laura works to ensure the firm's university relationships at the school level are coordinated with those strategies generated within the Americas Campus Recruiting Center of Expertise.

She started with Ernst & Young in May 2007, following a 15-year career in Higher Education as both an administrator and adjunct faculty member in Vermont, Massachusetts and, most recently, Upstate New York as Director of Corporate Relations for the Simon School of Business (University of Rochester). She's worked with both undergraduate and graduate students advising their career development and has taught students at the both the graduate and undergraduate levels.

Alan Muir

Alan is the Founding Executive Director of Career Opportunities for Students with Disabilities (COSD). COSD was founded after Alan joined the University of Tennessee (UT) in 1998. At that time, he recognized the disconnect between post-secondary offices of disability services and career services at universities across the country. With Dr. Bob Greenberg, then Director of Career Services at UT, he conducted research to document this anecdotal gap for the first time. Under his leadership, COSD experienced significant growth, bringing together member entities including universities, employers, and U.S. Government agencies to focus on career employment of college graduates with disabilities. He has presented at universities, employers and many conferences nationwide. Mr. Muir's previous business experience was as a Vice-President with Chase Manhattan Bank for 16 years.

Mr. Muir's outside involvement in disability and employment issues includes current memberships in Association of Higher Education and Disability (AHEAD), Tennessee AHEAD, National Association of Colleges and Employers (NACE) and the National Disability Mentorship Coalition.

In 2015, Mr. Muir was inducted into the Susan M. Daniels Disability Mentoring Hall of Fame as part of the initial class of 25 disability leaders in the 25th Anniversary of the Americans with Disabilities Act (ADA). In 2011, Mr. Muir received the Fred Strache Award for Leadership from the California State University Northridge (CSUN) Center on Disabilities at the 26th Annual Technology and Persons with Disabilities Conference. Mr. Muir also was the recipient of the 2004 AAPD / Paul G. Hearne Leadership Award, a distinguished and highly competitive national honor. Community service involvement includes membership on the Delta Air Lines National Advisory Board on Disability and the Board of Directors of Disability Rights Tennessee in Nashville, TN.

Lindsey Pollak

Lindsey Pollak is recognized as one of the leading experts on the Millennial generation in higher education and the workplace. Often called a "translator," Lindsey advises both young professionals looking to succeed in today's work environment and the organizations that want to recruit, retain and engage them. She is the New York Times best-selling author of two books, *Becoming the Boss: New Rules for the Next Generation of Leaders* and *Getting From College to Career: Your Essential Guide to Succeeding in the Real World.* She served for six years as an official Ambassador for LinkedIn, where she trained over 100,000 professionals in how to use the network. Lindsey's speaking audiences and consulting clients have included over 200 corporations, law firms, universities and business schools, including Citigroup, Dell, Estee Lauder, GE, JP Morgan, PricewaterhouseCoopers, Shearman & Sterling, Yale, Harvard, Wharton and MIT. Her advice and opinions have appeared in such media outlets as The TODAY Show, *The New York Times, The Wall Street Journal,* CNN and NPR. Lindsey is a graduate of Yale University and received a master's degree in women's studies from Monash University in Melbourne, Australia. She is based in New York City. Visit Lindsey's website at www.lindseypollak and follow her on Twitter @lindseypollak.

Bryan Quick

Bryan Quick has 20-plus years of leadership experience in talent acquisition and recruitment with multiple Fortune 100 companies. Bryan currently manages all recruitment for Abbott's global operations internship and professional development programs and is project manager for Abbott's STEM internship program. He was Director of Learning and Development at Lincoln Park Zoo prior to arriving at Abbott. Previously, he managed education operations at Disney's Animal Kingdom and managed training and development programs. He also provided leadership for recruitment efforts for Disney's college intern program which is one of the largest corporate internship programs in the world. Bryan holds a bachelor's degree in biology from Francis Marion University. Bryan has also held several positions for NACE and most recently served on the NACE Professional Development Advisory and Board of Directors Selection and Nomination committees.

Susan K. Reid

Susan is currently Managing Director, Human Resources and Global Head of Diversity and Inclusion for Morgan Stanley. She was formerly Managing Director of Human Resources with Marsh and McLennan and has prior experience in leading recruiting at both RR Donnelley and Bell Atlantic

(Verizon).

Susan has her degree in Economics and Political Science from New York University.

Steven Rothberg

Steven is the president and founder of College Recruiter, which believes that every student and recent graduate deserves a great career. College Recruiter is the leading job search engine for students and recent graduates of all one-, two-, and four-year colleges and universities. College Recruiter features well over 40,000 pages of articles, blogs, videos, and other content as well as hundreds of thousands of internship and entry-level job posting ads. Over the course of the year, College Recruiter helps almost three million students and recent graduates find employment.

Janine M. Rowe

Janine, MSEd., NCC, is a career counselor and Assistant Director of Disability Services at Rochester Institute of Technology in Rochester, NY. In addition to providing developmental career counseling, she provides education and advocacy for students with disabilities and consults with employers hiring individuals with disabilities. She obtained her master's degree in Counselor Education from The College at Brockport, SUNY. She has previously presented at NYSCDA, NCDA, and NACE Conferences and is the author of numerous articles regarding disability employment. She currently serves as the Vice President for New York State Career Development Association. Her professional interests include teaching, supervision, and developing creative ways to explore career development concepts.

Mary E. Scott

Mary is president of Scott Resource Group (www.ScottResourceGroup.com), a university relations and recruitment consulting firm based in West Hartford, Connecticut. Her professional services include client-specific primary research, student surveys, focus groups, best practices benchmarking studies and retention analysis. She provides professional services in university relations and recruitment to a client roster that has included some of the biggest and best-known employers in the nation, and is also a managing partner of IronHorse Surveys LLC, a provider of Web-based recruitment process assessment tools, including the IronHorse Index™ and Campus Brand Audit™ proprietary benchmarking survey instruments.

Prior to forming the Company in 1989, Mary served in a number of increasingly responsible positions as a recruitment professional Aetna Life & Casualty. As Director, Corporate Staffing, she had management responsibility for all Corporate Headquarters employment, as well as Aetna's national college relations and intern programs, information systems recruitment, temporary employee, and management development programs. Mary has additional recruitment experience as Assistant Director of Admissions at a private liberal arts college. She received her undergraduate degree in English from Saint Joseph College, West Hartford, Connecticut, and holds an MBA in Finance from the University of Connecticut.

Peggy Smith

Peggy Smith is President and Chief Executive Officer of Worldwide ERC®, the premier global organization for talent mobility and management. Peggy entered the mobility industry during her stellar career at Microsoft, where she expanded the company's workforce mobility reach from U.S. to global coverage. She was offered the CEO position at Worldwide ERC® in 2010, and since joining the organization, has shown that she is an experienced and innovative business leader and accomplished global strategist. She is recognized for her ability to build strong relationships with a range of professionals in workforce mobility, talent management, staffing, benefits, payroll, finance, and procurement. With a deep understanding of logistics, compliance, talent strategy and global economics, she brings an unwavering focus to the advancement of the workforce mobility industry. She has turned a practiced eye on expanding the association's footprint and educational program delivery in the APAC, EMEA and LATAM regions. Peggy holds a BA in marketing from Seattle University, as well as industry designations that include the Senior Certified Relocation Professional/SCRP® and the Senior Global Mobility Specialist/SGMS®-T. A frequent presenter at mobility and HR-related conferences around the world, Peggy has also guest-lectured on talent mobility at Georgetown University and Seattle University.

Bruce Soltys

Bruce currently leads the University Relations team at Travelers, a Dow 30 company and a leading provider of property casualty insurance for auto, home and business. The University Relations team is accountable for the design and delivery of the enterprise strategy for sourcing, attracting and recruiting a pool of diverse talent through relationships with targeted colleges, universities, and student organizations. Prior to Travelers, Bruce served as the Director of Campus Recruiting at Prudential and Manager of University Relations & Diversity Talent Partners at Verizon. He has held previous HR roles at Citi, EY and Lucent Technologies and obtained a Bachelors of Arts in Economics from Rutgers University. In addition to being a NACE member, he is a graduate of the NACE Leadership Advancement Program, serves as a NACE facilitator and has co-chaired a NACE committee focused on Professional Development. He will be joining the NACE Board of Directors for a 2-year term starting in July 2017. Outside of work, he enjoys running up mountains in the spring, summer and fall while skiing down them in the winter. A 3-time Ultra Marathoner, he resides in New Jersey.

Trudy Steinfeld

Trudy is currently the Associate Vice President and Executive Director of the New York University Wasserman Center for Career Development. She oversees over 50 full-time and 35 part-time staff.

Trudy has an extensive background in the field of career development, experiential education and recruiting and was selected to facilitate the training of external review consultants by the National Association of Colleges and Employers (NACE). Trudy was inducted into the NACE Academy of Fellows in 2015 and has co-chaired the Professional Employer Development Action Committee for NACE that development live and web based content for the recruiting community.

Trudy is currently a contributor to Forbes.com and writes a column entitled Career Warrior. She has served as a consultant to numerous colleges and universities, non-profits, and corporate recruiting organizations both within the United States and abroad. She recently co-edited and contributed to *Leadership in Career Services: Voices from the Field.* In addition, Trudy has been a presenter and keynote speaker at over 150 national meetings and conferences including the 2015 & 2016 NACE and NASPA national meetings, the 2014 SHRM New York program, the annual NACE Management Leadership Institute, WACE 2013 Global Meeting, NACE Social Media Mashups, Career Services Institute (CSI), Universum, and Women for Hire. She continues to chair and serve on several key committees, taskforces and major conferences for the National Association of Colleges and Employers (NACE), as well as having advised on several national conferences including the NACE Global Recruiting Symposium. In addition, Trudy has been a recipient of both NASPA and NACE Excellence awards.

Trudy is considered a national expert on the job market and employment trends and has been a frequent media contributor to: The New York Times, Wall Street Journal, Business Week, Fortune, New York Daily News, New York Post, Crain's, NBC, CBS, ABC, MTV, CNN, CNBC, MSNBC, NPR, CBS Radio, The Newshour with Jim Leher and several international television and print news outlets. Ms. Steinfeld was a featured career expert on the new cable show "The Job Hunt".

Trudy earned her Bachelor's degree in American Studies and Education from Ramapo College and holds a Master's degree from the Graduate School of Arts and Science at New York University. She has also completed extensive course work in Counseling Psychology from the NYU Steinhardt School of Culture, Education, and Human Development.

Graham Thompsett

Graham is currently Head of Talent Acquisition globally for Jaguar Land Rover based in Warwickshire in the United Kingdom, this is a new role from March 2015. In his new role, Graham is responsible for Future Talent (Grads/Under Grads & Apprentices), and all experienced hiring as well as Executive Hiring. Prior to this he spent 9 years in China carrying out three distinct projects for both Jaguar Land Rover and Ford Motor Company.

In 2006, he was responsible for developing the Ford Purchasing and Engineering Centre in Nanjing, China. The business grew from a staff of 40 to circa 400 in a two-year period and delivered significant returns to Ford Motor Company. He came back to JLR China when Ford sold Jaguar Land

Rover to TATA Motors. In 2009 Graham became Head of HR for Jaguar Land Rover in China and watched the business grow from selling 700 cars a year to well over 120,000 cars in 2014 – this was a key factor in the company's growth and success in the past six years. Graham's last role in China was to set a new Joint Venture production facility and business between Jaguar Land Rover and Chery Automotive and delivered it on time, on cost and on time. Prior to returning to the UK, Graham embarked on a project to build a joint venture in China between Chery Jaguar Land Rover and Chery Automotive. From March 2012 to March 2015, a business, a company culture, a factory and a vehicle were successfully launched – all firsts for Jaguar Land Rover.

Graham has held numerous senior Human Resources positions since joining Land Rover in 2001, including Head of Recruitment for JLR and also Head of Ford's external training in Europe. Passionate about Future Talent, Graham served for six years on the Board of the Association of Graduate Recruiters in the UK, a body which Jaguar Land Rover has supported for well over a decade.

Ayanna Naki Wilcher

Ayanna is the Diversity Recruiting Manager for the Mid-Atlantic region at KPMG. Ayanna joined the firm in November 2012. She has over 17 years of higher education experience and prior to KPMG, she spent eight years as the assistant director for Diversity & Career Development at Lehigh University and three years as the director of Minority Programs in the College of Engineering at Cornell University. For several years, she has been actively involved in Eastern Association of Colleges and Employers (EACE) and National Association of Colleges and Employers (NACE), where she served on the Board, presented on topics regarding diversity & recruitment and is serving as the 2015-2016 EACE President.

Ayanna is located in the Philadelphia office and her role in as the Mid-Atlantic Diversity recruiter is multifaceted. She works with the recruiting teams in the MD, DC, VA and PA offices in evaluating and improving the Diversity Strategies for locally important and premier schools. She also works the Campus Development Manager at Temple University and works closely with the Temple team to plan and execute events and identify the top students.

Ayanna is originally from Chicago, IL and received a BS degree in computer science from the University of Massachusetts and a MA degree in educational leadership from Lehigh University.

Shaunda Zilich

Shaunda has a passion in everything she does to impact people's lives…for the better of course. She does enjoy her career but she enjoys life more! She enjoys life everyday by not taking things too seriously, making people laugh, speaking at events, helping people learn from her mistakes and successes, volunteering to transform her community, taking part in local events (like the Bourbon Chase and music festivals), and more important than life itself is her faith and family.

Her passion to leave a positive impact on people's lives is why her role at GE as the Global Employment Brand Leader suits her well. As she puts it… 'she sells experiences, what can be better than that?'. Her 'past lives" include roles in marketing businesses and people in several industries. This has given her the experience outside of HR to do what she does today for GE. Four years ago, Shaunda started this adventure with GE to modernize its recruitment and bolster its employer brand. Now she runs a global team of three full-time employment brand leaders and a council of 35+ members, building employer branding across all functions and regions, in all GE businesses, and within all GE employees (big shoes!) Her 10+ years of experience in training professionals and companies on how to brand themselves have played a key role in her success at GE.